Strange Philadelphia

Strange Philadelphia

✳ *Stories from* ✳
the City of Brotherly Love

✳

Lou Harry

WITH THE ASSISTANCE OF
Michael Strickland

T TEMPLE UNIVERSITY PRESS

Temple University Press, Philadelphia 19122
Copyright © 1995 by Temple University
All rights reserved

Published 1995

Printed in the United States of America

Text designed by Judith Martin Waterman

LIBRARY OF CONGRESS CATALOGING-IN-PUBLICATION DATA
Harry, Lou, 1963–
    Strange Philadelphia : stories from the City of Broth-
erly Love / by Lou Harry : research assistance by Michael
Strickland.
    p.   cm.
    Includes bibliographical references (p.).
    ISBN 1-56639-375-2
    1. Philadelphia (Pa.)—History.   2. Curiosities and
wonders—Pennsylvania—Philadelphia.   3. Philadelphia
Region (Pa.)—History.   4. Curiosities and wonders—
Pennsylvania—Philadelphia Region.   I. Title.
F158.35.H37   1995
974.8'11—dc20   95-4769
                                              CIP

For Cindy,
who deserves epic novels and
volumes of poetry.
This will have to do for now.

CONTENTS

CONTENTS

CONTENTS ✵

CONTENTS

CONTENTS ✹

✄ ACKNOWLEDGMENTS ✄

Special thanks to Bill Tonelli, who allowed a green intern in a Goodwill suit the chance to research, then write, then develop as a column, the first batch of these pieces for *Philadelphia Magazine*; to my editor at Temple University Press, Doris Braendel, who helped turn the idea into a real live book; to Michael Strickland, an ace researcher who never complained; to computer ace Tim Haas, who has the strength of ten men; to Ginny Moles, editor of *Seven Arts* magazine, who gave me the breathing room to finish this book; and to George Brightbill at Temple University's Urban Achives, where many of these pieces were born. His assistance was invaluable.

Strange Philadelphia

Introduction
What Do You Mean, Strange?

My interest in Philadelphia-area strangeness began in 1986, when I was a new intern at *Philadelphia Magazine*. Bill Tonelli, then articles editor, wanted to satisfy readers of the magazine who had commented that they liked the magazine's pieces on local history. Fact was, though, *Philadelphia Magazine* rarely ran such articles, and Tonelli was trying to figure out a way to make history a minor but monthly part of the magazine's mix.

Of course I was interested in history, I told him, lying through my teeth.

The result was the first "Flashback" column that I wrote for the magazine—a piece about Brigadier General Smedley Darlington Butler, who came to town to clean up Philadelphia as police commissioner in 1923 and left in, well, read "A New Chief in Town, PART 2" and you'll see.

Unless noted, each story in this book was based on information gathered from news clipping files in Temple University's Urban Archives. Many of those previously appeared, in altered form, in *Philadelphia Magazine*.

1

Satisfied with that and two other pilot pieces, Tonelli gave me half a page of the magazine each month to tell a marginal tale from the region's past. Digging through fading news clips in the Temple University Urban Archives, checking for Philadelphia references in the indexes of any book I happened to pick up, and finding libraries in town I didn't know existed, my rather vague goal each month was to tell a true story that would make people's eyebrows rise.

The effect was greater than that on me, though. Smedley Butler not only opened the door to a freelance gig for me that lasted from mid-1986 into 1990, he also opened the door to history.

Being a high school student in the 1970s, I grew up with little passion for the subject. The textbooks were dull and the selection seemed random. We were a generation caught between "dates and places memorization" and today's thematic approach. The textbooks went up to the Vietnam War, but by the spring we hadn't even gotten to World War I. And nothing in the books convinced us that George Washington, Andrew Jackson, and the token minorities of history—Harriet Tubman, Pocahontas, and George Washington Carver—were actual human beings. Maybe it was the fact that everything they did seemed so important. Maybe it was post-Watergate frustration about the past and future on the part of the grownups around us. Maybe it was growing up in Wildwood, New Jersey, a resort town that, despite its wealth of tacky 1950s hotels, pretended to have no history whatsoever.

The only history books I can remember really grabbing me were Harlan Ellison's collections of television criticism for the L.A. *Free Press*, *The Glass Teat*, and *The Other Glass Teat*. These gritty, emotional volumes illustrated for me the day-to-day realities of what people were watching in the late 1960s and early 1970s and, more importantly, how these programs related to the political and social worlds around them.

As I dug through old news clippings in search of material for each month's "Flashback," I stumbled onto a similar world, a world that had been missing from the high school history books. By following these forgotten stories day to day in newspaper accounts, I found myself compelled by their drama, anxious to dig out the next day's edition on microfilm to see what happened next.

In the time between the start of the column and the completion of this book, I've discovered many history books that have excited me (although they have taken approaches radically different from mine). Any of them could have dramatically changed my attitudes toward history if I had discovered them earlier. I'm particularly fond of the work of Daniel J. Boorstin, former Librarian of Congress, who has skillfully combined telling details with a sense of the big picture in *The Americans* trilogy and, more globally, in *The Creators* and *The Explorers*. More playfully, Richard Shenkman's *Legends, Lies & Cherished Myths of American History* takes a delight in debunking the wealth of misinformation we pass along. *Philadelphia: A 300-Year History* offers much in the way of geographically focused history, and Howard Zinn's *A People's History of the United States* taught me to look beyond the headlines. All of these, even if not cited specifically in this book, have helped formed in me a layperson's curiosity about history.

In the preface to *Still Philadelphia*, a remarkable book of photography that not only helped put faces on the past for me but also led me to pitch *Strange Philadelphia* to Temple University Press, the trio of authors say that "[o]n one level, this is a Philadelphia family album." Well, if their volume is a family album, then *Strange Philadelphia* is the box of yellowed photos and news clips that didn't make it into the album. Still, for each of the *Philadelphia Magazine* columns—and for the seventy or so additional items in this book, I looked not for lasting influence, or for a politically correct ethnic mix, or for positive role models, but for something that made the incident or person, for better or worse, transcend the everyday. Sometimes that meant evoking a bizarre image, like a man scaling the side of City Hall or a floating bridge drifting down the Schuylkill River. Sometimes it meant finding offbeat information about familiar characters like Benjamin Rush and Benjamin Franklin. Sometimes it meant reviving the memories of now forgotten but once popular figures such as Octavius Catto and Richard Vaux.

What most of these incidents share is the fact that they've been discarded by history. Scandals are forgotten, mayors are forgotten, front-page news is forgotten, colorful characters that everyone in town knew are forgotten, hoaxes that affected hundreds are forgotten. In the realm of history, it is survival of the fittest. Each year, more and more history is created. Each year, more trivia fills our heads. Each year, we forget more of the past.

That's the reality of historical Darwinism. There's only so much material that can be carried from one generation's living room to be crated and stored in the next generation's attic. We must, for our own sanity, let once well-known stories slip into the realm of the forgotten simply because they didn't happen to be the things that helped us significantly in getting where we are. Or because they were embarrassing. Or because they didn't fit into the myth we've collectively created.

The initial effect of rediscovering these items may be curiosity and amusement, but there's often a more important result. Together, they illuminate the fact that our ancestors were painfully human beings. To a generation too cynical to put history on a pedestal by memorizing names, dates, and places, yet too busy to study it any other way, I think that's a significant realization. "Strange," to me, is not a term that carries with it a value judgment. There is an infinite variety of strangeness, from the innocent to the evil. The skin experiments of Dr. Thomas Eldridge are of a drastically different order from the birth of the Slinky. A western shot live on City Line Avenue has little in common with a cross-dressing AWOL World War II soldier/magician. In the same way that we can look at colonial cookware at the Atwater Kent Museum and gain insight into life long before our births, so too history buffs and the mildly curious will find something in this book that reverberates with a faint cry of "That was us back then." As we face off with a new generation of mass murderers, mayoral misconduct allegations, and migrations to Jersey to see the Virgin Mary appear in a tree, we often forget past variations on these same themes.

For these items, I found leads in dozens of places—from a mention of Catto in an exhibition at the Atwater Kent Museum to a bad movie at the local video store called *The Philadelphia Experiment*. Journalistic colleagues gave me tips. . . . so did my barber. Getting to the real story meant digging through materials at the Philadelphia Free Library, the Library Company of Philadelphia, and other Delaware Valley facilities.

Once I started actively looking, I found a wealth of twentieth-century material in Temple University's Urban Archives. Here were stories that made the headlines in their day. Ask around about the Palace of Depression, the Keely Motor hoax, and Ben Franklin's human electrical experiments. Listen to a city give a collective "huh?" (You'll probably get the same response if you ask for four signers of the Declaration of Independence, but that's another, more depressing, story). Recent strange cases, like those of Jeffrey Dahmer, Tonya Dacrei, and Eddie Savitz have grabbed Philadelphia's attention and are still green in the city's memory, but I've opted to pass on the city's recent nightmares. Let history deal with them first.

The toughest thing about writing this book was stopping. New stories came to my attention even as I approached my deadline and I'm sure there are many more out there. I deliberately held back on recent events to allow them time to be distilled by history. But I would love to hear more stories or follow up on leads you may have for future editions or sequels to *Strange Philadelphia*.

Hints on additional strange Philadelphia anecdotes can be sent to Lou Harry c/o Temple University Press, Broad and Oxford Streets, Philadelphia, PA 19122. ✖

The Deal

1683

The image is familiar to anyone who ever wandered through the Pennsylvania Academy of the Fine Arts or shopped at Strawbridge and Clothier stores—a guy in colonial garb reaching a hand out to a group of Native Americans. But contrary to the scene depicted on the S&C logo and in Benjamin West's famous painting *William Penn's Treaty with the Indians*, William Penn himself was not on hand to bargain with the Native Americans in 1683 for the land that would become Phila-delphia.

Penn was actually home back in England taking care of business, leaving the treaty to his representatives. Led by City Council head Thomas Holmes, the Europeans met with the Leni Lenape tribe, represented by Secane, Shakkoppoh, Malibore, and Tangoras, and struck a deal that included two hundred fathom of wampum, and such unusual but practical items as thirty pairs of hawks' bells, thirty pairs of stockings, twelve pairs of hose, and thirty combs. 🦋

Penn's Witch
1683

They said Margaret Mattson was a witch. They said that, although oxen may have been above the "malignant powers," cattle were in grave danger. Colonists feared her, which is why the Swedish native was brought before a panel of judges, led by Governor William Penn. The charge against Mattson was that she had violated a law, carried over from King James I, which stated that it was illegal to commit "conjuration, witchcraft and dealing with evil and wicked spirits."

She pleaded not guilty and the parade of witnesses began. According to the *Minutes of the Provincial Council of Pennsylvania*:

> Henry Drystreet attested, Saith he was told 20 years ago, that the prisoner at the Barr was a Witch, & that several Cows were bewitcht by her; also that James Saunderling's mother told him that she bewitcht her cow.

Minutes of the Provincial Council of Pennsylvania, vol. 1. (1852), pp. 94–97. J. F. Watson, *Annals of Philadelphia, and Pennsylvania, in the Olden Times* (1927), pp. 265–266, 274.

Hardly damning evidence. But there was more.

Charles Ashcom, the next witness, gave a confusing story in which the most damaging point was that Mattson's daughter had called on him, claiming to have seen a great light and an old woman with a knife at the foot of her bed.

Later, Annakey Coolin attested that her husband took the

> heart of a Calfe that Dyed, as they thought, by Witchcraft, and Boyled it, whereupon [Mattson] came in and asked them what they were doing; they said boyling of flesh; she said they had better they had Boyled the Bones with several other unseemly Expressions.

"The Prisoner denyeth all things," stated the minutes, "and saith that ye Witnesses speake only by hear say."

The jury was charged by Penn to come back with a verdict. Instead, they returned from deliberations with a mixed message not unfamiliar to students of twentieth-century jury hedging. They found her "guilty of having the common fame of a witch, but not guilty in the manner and form as she stands indicted."

The punishment? A security of fifty pounds paid by Mattson and her codefendant Yeshro Hendrickson to secure their good behavior for the next six months. No trouble was registered again from Mattson and the next council meeting took on a more serious matter—"a Notorious Robery committed on the Goods of hannah Saulter."

The End Is Near, PART 1
1694

Johann Jacob Zimmerman, mathematician, astronomer, and theologian, had done some calculating. The way he figured it, the millennium would begin in the fall of 1694. In Württemberg, he gathered a group of believers and made plans to set out for America, but he died just before the ship's departure.

The group was taken over by John Kelpius, former chaplain to the Prince of Denmark. They arrived in Maryland in June, then proceeded to Germantown, where they settled on a ridge overlooking the Wissahickon Creek.

There, Kelpius became known as "the hermit on the ridge" as he and his followers built log houses and waited . . . and waited . . . and waited for "the woman of the wilderness" to appear and bring about the end of the world.

She never did.

J. F. Watson, *Annals of Philadelphia, and Pennsylvania, in the Olden Times* (1927), pp. 458–460. Joseph Jackson, *Encyclopedia of Philadelphia* (Harrisburg, Pa.: Harrisburg National Historical Association, 1932), pp. 805–806.

Please, Mr. Postman

1737

A mong Ben Franklin's many achievements is often listed his stint as Postmaster of Philadelphia and as Deputy Postmaster General for the American colonies from 1753 to 1774. During that time, Franklin managed to turn the post office into a successful, money-making entity.

But altruism was not the only thing on Franklin's mind. He also quickly established the post office as a means to his own business ends.

Franklin knew that there were no rules specifying anyone's right to send newspapers by mail. And since no rates were firmly established, Franklin simply ignored rival printers' requests for mailing privileges. Instead he loaded down the mail carriers with his own papers and enjoyed the use of a private delivery system that cut off the competition.

"It facilitated the correspondence that improv'd my newspaper, increas'd the number demanded, as well as the advertisements to be inserted, so that it came to afford me a considerable income," said Franklin with unashamed candor. "My old competitor's declin'd proportionately."

Daniel J. Boorstin, *The Americans: The Colonial Experience* (New York, Random House: 1958), pp. 338.

The Caveman, PART 1

1741

John Key, the first child born of English parents in Philadelphia, was born in a cave. Thomas Wynne, Philadelphia's first doctor, lived in a cave. Such was the nature of seventeenth-century colonization, when the soft, dry banks of the Delaware River provided relatively easy homemaking. Part of William Penn's original plan for Philadelphia was that caves should be used for dwellings only for the first three years of colonization—until 1685. But the following year, despite Penn's decree, there were still so many occupied caves that Penn, back in England once again, sent word that they should all be demolished.

"That you shutt up ye caves of Philadelphia to prevent clandestine loosness and stir up ye Magistrates to minde sobriety there," wrote Penn.

Around the same time, a man who would later become Philadelphia's most famous cave dweller was born. His name was Benjamin Lay.

Born of a good Quaker family in the 1680s in En-

Carl Sifakis, *Great American Eccentrics: Strange and Peculiar People* (New York: Galahad Books, 1984), pp. 15-18.

gland, Lay became a sailor, despite his height of only four feet, seven inches, and boarded a ship while in his twenties. His stint at sea lasted all of seven years but came to a halt when his Quaker ideals came in contact with the mores of his fellow sailors (this was long before the Tailhook scandal) and he quit in a huff.

Returning to London, Lay married, but his hot temper repeatedly got him into trouble, leading to two expulsions from Quaker meetings. He and his wife then moved to Barbados, where he became both a vegetarian (after having witnessed the slaughter of animals) and a passionate anti-slavery speaker. This was not a popular position among the many slaveholders on the island. Lay soon relocated once more, this time to Philadelphia, a place where he was again repulsed by the rampant slavery.

Next stop—the suburbs.

His new residence was a cave, albeit one with some then-modern conveniences . . . like furniture. From this base of operations on York Road, Lay made a nuisance of himself at the downtown Market Street meeting. On one occasion, he was ejected from a Quaker meeting and stayed where he had fallen in the gutter until the end of the meeting, forcing his fellow Quakers to walk over him.

"Can I help you?" asked one departing Quaker.

"No," answered Lay, "Let those who cast me here raise me up. It is their business, not mine."

Lay stayed in his cave until 1741, when sickness forced him to leave. While living with friends in Abington, his wife died, leaving him alone to rant and pursue his other hobby, making beehives. On his deathbed, Lay heard that the Society of Friends had voted to put all slaveholders out of their meeting. Lay is said to have shouted, "Hallelujah, I can now die in peace."

Lay's legend lived, at least for a while, and portraits of him in front of his cave became popular in Quaker households throughout Philadelphia. The caption under his bearded likeness read:

> Benjamin Lay, Lived to the Age of 80, in the Latter Part of Which he Observed extreme Temperance in his Eating and Drinking, his Fondness for the Particularity in Dress and Customs at times Subjected him to Ridicule of the Ignorant, but his Friends who were Intimate with him Thought him an Honest Religious Man. ✂

Ben's Off-Color Advice

1745

In a 1745 letter to a friend, Benjamin Franklin recommended that a young man should opt for an older woman instead of a younger one because, among other things, "They are so grateful!" Besides, Franklin added, "Below the girdle, it is impossible to tell an old one from a younger one."

According to revisionist historian Richard Shenkman, "If we do not know much about the cosmopolitan Franklin it is because our image of Franklin was shaped by the Victorians, and Victorians did not cotton to the idea of the rakish founding father."

Roast Turkey

1750

Ben Franklin's legendary experiment with the kite, the key, and lightning (in which, many historians note, he actually sent his son out into the storm, to avoid his own public embarrassment) was but one in a series of his unusual electrical exercises. For several years before he (or his son) raised the kite, Franklin, who was already praised throughout the Western world as an inventor and printer, had been performing some weird scientific experiments that involved electrocutions of barnyard fowl.

He used humans, too—in non-fatal experiments. Once he lined up six men, each with a hand on the next man's forehead. The last man in line held a chain connected to a pair of battery jars. Franklin held one end of a metal rod to a conductor and touched the other end to the head of the first man in line. The result, according to Franklin's letters:

> A person so struck sinks down doubled, or folded together as it were, the joints losing their strength and stiffness at once, so that he drops on the spot where he stood.

18

Franklin was intrigued that the men neither swayed nor fell longways when they went down, and from this experiment he realized that it would be both possible and practical to kill a person using electricity. It would be, he concluded, "the easiest of all deaths."

His notebooks from 1749 listed several similarities between lightning and electricity, one of which was that both were capable of "destroying animals." He proved that many times in the following year, when he discovered, among other things, that a lot more voltage was necessary to kill a turkey than a chicken, and that when either bird is killed in this manner, it is "uncommonly tender" when eaten.

Perhaps his most important lesson came two days before Christmas in 1750. Momentarily distracted by the presence of admirers in his lab, Franklin mistakenly attached himself rather than his intended victim, a turkey, to the hot end of his apparatus. The resulting jolt was strong enough to knock Franklin to the floor, giving him a lump on the head "the bigness of half a swan shot or pistol bullet." He thus discovered that a man could withstand a far greater electrical shock than had previously been thought possible.

There is no record of what happened to that particular bird. But years later, Franklin, perhaps by way of apology, proposed the turkey be named to the coveted position of "national bird," a symbol for the new country.

The proposal was defeated. ✄

The Town of Bath

1765

Pre-revolutionary Philadelphia housed a number of mineral springs, which some physicians advocated to keep their patients healthy.

John White decided to cash in on the craze by creating his own health resort, called Town of Bath, at his Northern Liberties farm along Cohocksink Creek. He hoped health-conscious Philadelphians would flock to his farm to take cold baths, drink mineral water, eat good food, and escape the foul air of city life a few blocks away.

He advertised this Town of Bath in the *Pennsylvania Gazette* in August 1765, but got only as far as erecting a small bath house over a spring and hanging a sign on his farmhouse. 🦋

David Armstrong and Elizabeth Metzger Armstrong, *The Great American Medicine Show: Being an Illustrated History of Hucksters, Healers, Health Evangelists, and Heroes from Plymouth Rock to the Present* (Englewood Cliffs, N.J., 1991), p. 186.

The Philadelphia
Tea Party
1773

I n 1773, word reached Philadelphia that King George III had granted exclusive American importing rights to the East Indian Tea Company of London. A meeting was held in the State House and an angry resolution was written warning the tea company that any ships docking at the Delaware River port would be burned.

A copy of the resolution was sent to Boston.

Ignoring the warnings, four ships arrived in America, three in Boston, one in Philadelphia. The Boston Tea Party was the result of the first delivery. The unheralded Philadelphia version went differently.

Captain Ayers of the Philadelphia-bound *Polly* was docked for what he thought was a simple delivery to Thomas Wharton. Instead, Ayers was met in Chester by a gang of "escorts" who sent him across the river to Gloucester and then to Philadelphia, where he was taken to the State House. According to estimates, a quarter of the city's population showed up to witness Ayers being presented with a document signed by The Committee for Tar and Feathering.

The wise captain took the locals seriously and turned his ship around and headed back for England. ✄

The Floating Bridge
1776

I n 1780, the icy Schuylkill River carried away Philadelphia's only floating bridge.

The structure, spanning the river at Market Street, had a history dating back to 1776, when General Israel Putnam, the man militarily in charge of Philadelphia, ordered a bridge to be built from ship carpenter's floating stages, which were usually used for graving ships.

The following year, the bridge was replaced by a different floating one. After the Battle of Brandywine in 1777, the bridge was removed from the river and stored until the British evacuated the city.

After the bridge's 1780 exit, it was caught, fixed, and returned, but only until a 1789 flood swept it away for good. 🦋

Joseph Jackson, *Encyclopedia of Philadelphia* (Harrisburg, Pa.: Harrisburg National Historical Association, 1932), pp. 668, 857–871.

Burned on the
Fourth of July
1776

The Declaration of Independence was signed without much excitement in Philadelphia since it had already been published two days earlier in the *Pennsylvania Evening Post.* That night, though, thirteen cannons were fired from each of the ships in the navy, thirteen rockets shot up from the commons, the coat-of-arms of King George III was removed from the State House and burned, and a band of captured Hessian soldiers played patriotic music while notables gathered in the City Tavern making toasts to liberty.

Thus began a longstanding tradition of raucous holiday celebrations. Nearly a hundred years later, a Philadelphia diary noted that the tradition of mixing fire with the Independence Day continued. "As a general rule thirty or forty houses are set afire every 4th of July."

The Fort Wilson Affair

1778

Born in Scotland in 1742 and educated at St. Andrew's College and Edinburgh University, James Wilson emigrated to Philadelphia and, after studying law with John Dickerson, was admitted to the bar in 1767. He became Carlisle, Pennsylvania's leading citizen and a signer of the Declaration of Independence. He died in 1798 while visiting a friend in North Carolina, and in 1906 his body was reinterred at Christ Church in Philadelphia.

But his condensed history usually skips the fact that Philadelphia wasn't always a hospitable place for Wilson. In one particularly unpleasant instance, his house at Third and Walnut streets was attacked by his fellow Philadelphians in an intense display of post-Revolutionary reactionism.

The attack arose out of a movement against "monopolists" and "engrossers," words used to describe anyone believed to have been helpful to the enemy during the British occupation of the city. A committee appointed to investigate and obtain evidence against such sympathizers to the crown came up with an enemies list, which was posted in October

Joseph Jackson, *Encyclopedia of Philadelphia* (Harrisburg, Pa.: Harrisburg National Historical Association, 1932), pp. 678–679.

1778. James Wilson was one of the unfortunates who found his name was on it. It seems that Wilson, in his capacity as a lawyer, had represented some Tories in legal actions. This did not sit well with the committee, which held another meeting at Mrs. Burns's Tavern. A crowd of about two hundred picked a leader and then marched toward City Tavern, where they assumed Wilson would be hanging out.

But he wasn't. The armed mob, undaunted, headed for Wilson's house on Third Street. This time they found him. Wilson was home, entertaining a group of prominent citizens, including Robert Morris (whose name was also on the list), Captain Campbell, and General Mifflin.

Campbell took the initiative. He opened a window on the third floor and had a brief conversation with someone in the mob. It didn't go well. In what would prove to be a major miscalculation, Campbell shook his pistol in the air in defiance of the gang. The mob was not thrilled. They were even less impressed when Campbell fired his weapon. The rioters returned fire and collectively decided to try to get into the house. Wilson's door was broken with a sledge hammer. Colonel Stephen Chambers made the mistake of going to the door. In a resulting fight, Chambers was stabbed with a bayonet.

The noise attracted the Philadelphia Light Horse cavalry. Arrests, injuries, and two deaths resulted before the crowd was dispersed. ✼

Arnold's Debt
1778

In 1778, George Washington appointed Benedict Arnold commander of Philadelphia after the British had evacuated the city. Arnold moved into the Mount Pleasant Estate in Fairmount Park, married Peggy Shippen, the "darling of Philadelphia society," and ran into trouble with civil authorities for consorting with ladies of Loyalist sympathies, among other offenses. An inconclusive court-martial resulted.

Two years later, when Arnold's infamous plan to turn West Point over to the British was discovered, his wife returned to Philadelphia but was ordered out. The couple moved back to England, leaving behind a stunned country and their overdue mortgage payments.

Up, Up, and Away,

PART 1

1783

I f you were following the development of aeronautics and you happened to live in France in the late 1700s, you'd have believed that Philadelphia was the site of America's first balloon ascension. It happened, a Parisian paper noted, on December 28, 1783.

The flyer, James Wilcox, was said to have gone up in his own creation, which was rigged with forty-seven small balloons. The flight lasted five minutes, when Wilcox popped some of the balloons to keep from flying over the Schuylkill River.

Or so the papers reported. The whole affair was later discovered to be a hoax. According to William Trimble, author of *High Frontier: A History of Aeronautics in Pennsylvania*, the sham was most likely led by two of Philadelphia's leading citizens, David Rittenhouse and Francis Hopkinson, who intended it as a way of pulling the legs of balloon-mad Europeans. ❧

William F. Trimble, *High Frontier: A History of Aeronautics in Pennsylvania* (Pittsburgh: University of Pittsburgh Press, 1982), p. 5.

Up, Up, and Away,

PART 2

1784

D r. John Foulke, a graduate of the University of Pennsylvania, had studied early flight experiments in Paris while completing his medical studies there. On May 10, 1784, he let loose a small paper hot air balloon from the courtyard of the Dutch minister's residence, thus launching the first recorded balloon flight in America. The next day, he launched the second from the home of the French minister.

Inspired by Foulke's work, and backed by the American Philosophical Society, physician Dr. John Morgan tried to raise money to build a larger balloon than the one floated by Foulke. He advertised in the *Pennsylvania Gazette* for investors in "a large and elegant Air Balloon" to be sixty feet high. Without enough takers, the project never got off the ground.

But that summer, another would-be aviator entered the picture. Peter A. Carnes and a partner were coming off

William F. Trimble, *High Frontier: A History of Aeronautics in Pennsylvania* (Pittsburgh: University of Pittsburgh Press, 1982), p. 5.

the brief success of a Baltimore flight, but Carnes wanted to try one on his own. On July 17, with an estimated ten thousand Philadelphians looking on, Carnes's balloon began to rise from the city's prison yard. The joyful cries of the crowd were soon cut short by a gust of wind that knocked the balloon against the prison wall. Carnes fell from the wicker basket, the balloon continued to rise and, at about a thousand feet from the ground, caught fire and plummeted to the ground.

After the incident, Carnes was significantly less enthusiastic about leaving the ground.   ✺

Citizen Genêt

1793

The most celebrated visitor to Philadelphia in 1793 was Edmond Charles Genêt, minister plenipotentiary and consul general of the French Republic.

Feeling a kinship with those who fought the French Revolution, Americans embraced the visit by Genêt and treated him, although they probably wouldn't have chosen the term, like a king.

Genêt made his American landing in Charleston, South Carolina, and headed north toward Philadelphia. So excited were Philadelphians (who had taken to imitating the French by calling each other "Citizen") that they sent the city's fastest horses down South and back to keep up a constant stream of news of Genêt's trip.

But Genêt's stay in Philadelphia wasn't celebrated by everyone. Although he was given two banquets at Oeller's Tavern on Chestnut Street, his behavior did not thrill governing officials who were more aware of his motives. Genêt was trying to recruit Americans to fight as seamen on French ships and as soldiers in British Canada and Spanish Louisi-

Joseph Jackson, *Encyclopedia of Philadelphia* (Harrisburg, Pa.: Harrisburg National Historical Association, 1932), p. 719.

ana. He was also looking for money—$2 million—that he claimed the United States owed France.

Thomas Jefferson tried to explain to him that Senate approval was necessary for such an action, and that the Senate was not meeting again until autumn (it was May when he arrived). Alexander Hamilton, Secretary of the Treasury, told him the treasury was empty. George Washington reacted coldly.

Genêt wasn't happy with the reaction. He continued to search for privateers and threatened to rally the American people to revolt.

In August, a note was sent to France to recall its minister. In February of the following year, a successor arrived. Genêt moved to New York, married the daughter of Governor Clinton, and drifted into obscurity. ✦

Up, Up, and Away,

PART 3

1793

Balloon success in Philadelphia was ultimately achieved by Jean Pierre Blanchard, the first to cross the English Channel by air. On January 9, 1793, crowds gathered—at $2 to $5 a person—at Sixth and Walnut to observe Blanchard's American take-off. President George Washington, a sponsor of the project, was on hand and watched as the balloon lifted off smoothly from Philadelphia. It arrived safely forty-six minutes later in Gloucester County, New Jersey.

There was a problem, though, that tempered Blanchard's excitement over his historical achievement. He did not make any money from his flight.

Afterward, Blanchard tried to make up the loss by setting up his balloon on Chestnut Street and charging the curious twenty-five cents to watch his balloon being inflated. There were few takers, so a second flight was planned.

William F. Trimble, *High Frontier: A History of Aeronautics in Pennsylvania* (Pittsburgh: University of Pittsburgh Press, 1982), pp. 6–7.

This time, vandals damaged the craft before it could be launched.

By June, Blanchard was getting desperate. He resorted to experimenting on animals, sending a cat, a dog, and a squirrel on an incredible journey to what he hoped would be the delight of paying customers. Again, few came to watch. He tried another animal cruise twelve days later but again the crowd was sparse.

Getting the hint, and unable to raise money for another manned flight, Blanchard left Philadelphia in a huff. ✹

Rush's Good
Intentions, PART 1
1793

President Washington got out of town. So did members of his cabinet. So did most of wealthy Philadelphia. Left were the poor and the sick.

No, it wasn't Memorial Day weekend. It was the yellow fever epidemic of 1793. Speculation spread quickly that the dreaded disease, which was killing up to twenty-four people a day, was caused by a load of coffee from Santo Domingo that was rotting on an Arch Street wharf. While Mayor Matthew Clarkson ordered the coffee cleared away, Dr. Benjamin Rush began searching for ways to help the victims.

Rush was a signer of the Declaration of Independence and one of the country's leading physicians. This wasn't saying much, considering a standard course of study in medical school lasted sixteen to twenty weeks and

David Armstrong and Elizabeth Metzger Armstrong, *The Great American Medicine Show: Being an Illustrated History of Hucksters, Healers, Health Evangelists, and Heroes from Plymouth Rock to the Present* (Englewood Cliffs, N.J., 1991), pp. 1–6.

admission only required a high school diploma and payment of a fee.

Rush had heard that an outbreak of yellow fever had swept the city of Charleston, South Carolina, without affecting that city's large black population. This led Rush, a noted abolitionist, to the belief that Philadelphia blacks would not be at risk. Thus, he encouraged whites to employ blacks as nurses. At the same time, he let blacks know that helping the dying white population would be a great step toward racial harmony. He even suggested to Richard Allen, the leader of Mother Bethel, the founding church of black Methodists, that the outbreak might be part of some divine plan.

The Free Africa Society Allen had cofounded and the black Methodist and Episcopal churches took up the cause. They enlisted members of their organizations and asked Mayor Clarkson to release all Philadelphia prisoners who agreed to act as nurses.

Allen joined Rush in overseeing the nurses, and other blacks supervised the burial detail. It soon became clear that they were far from immune to the sickness, but this, however, did not deter them from continuing their efforts. By the time the outbreak ended, more than two hundred blacks had died.

Mathew Carey, author of *A Short Account of the Malignant Fever, Lately Prevalent in Philadelphia*, published in 1793, told how the nurses faithfully carried out their duties. But he also repeated the popular allegation among the city's whites that some caretakers had extorted high fees and had robbed the homes of the wealthy.

Allen and Absalom Jones countered with their own document, *A Narrative of the Proceedings of the Black People During the Late Awful Calamity*, which presented their version of events. "Were poor blacks at fault," they asked, "if they accepted high wages freely offered by whites?"

Besides, Carey himself didn't witness the acts he described. He had abandoned the city as soon as the epidemic began. 🦋

Rush's Good Intentions, PART 2

1799

D r. Benjamin Rush was a member of the team of physicians that attended to George Washington on his deathbed at Mount Vernon. Among the treatments prescribed by Rush to cure the ailing president were:

➤ extensive bleeding by piercing the skin with a lancet and allowing thirty-two ounces of blood to drain into cups;

➤ wheat bran applied to his legs;

➤ administration of calomel, a mercury chloride powder, to empty his bowels; and

➤ blistering the skin to draw off liquids.

Washington died on December 14, 1799, shortly after he had begun treatment. 🦋

Live on Stage
1807–1813

In the early 1800s, the entertainment dollars of Philadelphia citizens went in some strange directions.

For example, advertisements posted for one of 1809's top attractions in Philadelphia read: "An astonishing female artist."

It was Miss Sarah, a young woman with no arms and no legs who brought her act to the Shakespeare Hotel at Sixth and Chestnut streets. Visitors gawked while she used her mouth to paint flowers, thread a needle, and cut cloth with scissors.

In 1811, interest shifted to Zerah Colburn, the six-year-old "calculator boy" from Vermont. At various locations throughout the city, including Peale's Model Room on 5th Street, Colburn would complete complicated mathematical problems for a paying crowd. According to his memoir,

In . . . Philadelphia the reception he met with was

Zerah Colburn, *A Memoir of Zerah Colburn, Written by Himself* (1833), pp. 10–11. Charles Coleman Sellers, *Mr. Peale's Museum: Charles Wilson Peale and the First Popular Museum of Natural Science and Art* (1804), p. 216.

very flattering, the inhabitants signifying their approbation of his talent by liberal attendance and donations . . . a likeness of him was taken by Rembrandt Peale and placed in the gallery of the museum.

Wax museums were another source of interest and amusement, with the displays often depicting unusual sights. Jesse Sharpless opened his wax museum in 1807. Among his dioramas were, according to an advertisement

a figure showing the muscles, etc., of the human body, the head of John the Baptist on a charger, a calf with two heads, six legs and two tails, Othello stabbing Desdemona [ignoring Shakespeare, in whose play Othello smothers her], O'Brian McCool, the Irish Giant, weighing seven hundred pounds, and a correct likeness of philosopher Richard Folwell.

Not to be outdone, the Washington Museum and Gallery of Painting, also on Market Street, featured:

General Moreau, who joined the Emperor of Russia against Bonaparte, after he was dreadfully wounded by a cannon ball. . . . His thigh bone is plainly to be seen . . his countenance exhibiting the pallid hue of death.

Added, in 1820, were "several French, English, and American dandies."

The Dyott Deception

1810

T homas Dyott was polishing shoes for a living in the 1810s when he saw the road to fortune. Following in the tradition of Pennsylvanians Thomas and Sybilla Masters (who, in 1715, used the first patent granted by England in the colonies to create the first American patent medicines), he came up with a line of "family remedies," including Robertson's Infallible Worm Destroying Lozenges.

This was a time when the public was bombarded by unregulated concoctions that promised to cure all ills for a few pennies. To separate a product from the competition, false pedigrees were often created and Dyott knew a little something about this misleading marketing technique. He claimed that his medicated marvels were developed by a "Dr. Robertson of Edinburgh."

It didn't take long for it to be discovered that no Dr.

David Armstrong and Elizabeth Metzger Armstrong, *The Great American Medicine Show: Being an Illustrated History of Hucksters, Healers, Health Evangelists, and Heroes from Plymouth Rock to the Present* (Englewood Cliffs, N.J., 1991), p. 163.

Robertson had, in the past two centuries, practiced medicine in Edinburgh. But Dyott went along undaunted. He expanded to other cities and declared himself a doctor of medicine, a move that boosted sales even further. Dyott, who was making up to $250,000 a year from his bottles of bunk, bought the Kensington Glass Works on the Delaware River and used it as a bottle-making facility.

The renamed Dyottville Glasswork facility, at peak, employed 450 workers who were not allowed to swear, gamble, or drink liquor. This wasn't too much of a problem for at least 225 of his workers were under eight years old. But the rest, too, had no choice but to accept Dyott's rules or face unemployment. These residents of Dyottville had to bathe regularly and attend Sunday school or risk losing part of their paychecks.

Dyott's downfall came not from government regulation or journalistic investigation, but from his own attempts to control the lives of his workers. He started his own bank to handle his workers' money, but in the panic of 1839, it hit hard times. He filed for bankruptcy and, in the resulting investigation, it was discovered that Dyott had distributed stock to his relatives before filing for Chapter 11. He was convicted and sentenced to jail for fraudulent insolvency. ✹

A Mammoth
Theater War
1812

Philadelphia theater history has been romanticized as a world ruled by the great tragedians of Philadelphia—Edwin Forrest and the Barrymore clan. But in the early 1800s, the most popular entertainers couldn't handle Shakespeare, but they did have tough skin and impressive trunks.

Elephant-mania had been going on for years in Philadelphia. "Now or Never!" called an announcement in the *Aurora General Advertiser* in December 1812.

> A Living Elephant, To be seen at the Sign of the
> Sorrel Horse, North Second Street, No. 39. To Remain until January. The Elephant is not only the

William B. Wood, *Personal Recollections of the Stage Embracing Notices of Actors, Authors, and Auditors during a Period of Forty Years* (1855), pp. 171, 186. Joseph Jackson, *Encyclopedia of Philadelphia* (Harrisburg, Pa.: Harrisburg National Historical Association, 1932), pp. 107–108, 464. Reese D. James, *Old Drury of Philadelphia: A History of the Philadelphia Stage 1800–1835* (1932), pp. 114, 122, 344, 355, 480, 482. Advertisements in *Aurora General Advertiser*, December 12, 17, 19, 21, 28, 1812.

largest and most sagacious animal in the world, but from the peculiar manner in which it takes its food and drink of every kind with its trunk, is acknowledged to be the greatest natural curiosity ever offered to the public.

In December 1812, Chestnut Street Theatre comanager William Burke Wood recalled, "A learned elephant contributed in Philadelphia this season to the attraction of Blue Beard, now revived." Another account recalls how "on the Christmas holidays [an elephant] lent his portly presence to the plays *Barbarossa* and *The Forty Thieves*." A later event was billed as "*[The] Stranger & [The] Thieves* [For the benefit of the Proprietors of the Elephant.]"

A decade later, elephants were still in vogue. The Chestnut, affectionately known as Old Drury, announced that

in the course of [*The Forty Thieves*] will appear a Living Elephant, (the largest animal of the kind ever exhibited in America), superbly caparisoned, with Riders . . . in the Asiatic style.

But the most controversial pachyderm performer was surely D'Jick, a beast who was caught in an unusual contractual court battle. It seems both the Arch Street Theatre and Old Drury believed they had D'Jick under contract for performances on the same evening in January 1831. Patrons at the Arch Street Theater were in their seats waiting for the show to start while, in the courtroom, Judge Hopkinson heard the Chestnut's plea for an injunction, claiming that they had a previous understanding with Mr. Gallot, the elephant's master. The judge refused, and D'Jick appeared at the Arch.

Thomas Jefferson Wrote Here

1824

The Marquis de Lafayette visited the United States with a mission—to seek out places important to the American Revolution. To his surprise, no one was quite sure where Thomas Jefferson wrote the Declaration of Independence. To resolve the debate, noted linguist Daniel Webster visited Jefferson at Monticello in 1824. Webster's encounter was recorded by the wife of Jefferson's companion, who said it was written "in a house on the north side of Chestnut Street between Third and Fourth. . . . Heiskell's Tavern in Fourth Street has been shown for it to Mr. Webster, but this is not the house."

Unsatisfied, Dr. James Mease, author of *Picture of Philadelphia in 1810*, wrote to the former president in search of an answer. Jefferson wrote back that he had lodged at the house of a "Mr. Graaf." He meant Jacob Graff, Jr. "I think he was a bricklayer," wrote Jefferson, "and that his house was on the South side of Market Street, probably between Seventh and Eighth Streets."

Silvio A. Bedini, *Declaration of Independence Desk: Relic of Revolution* (Washington, D.C.: Smithsonian Institution Press, 1981).

Six weeks later, Jefferson wrote again. "Your letter of September 8th . . . has excited my curiosity to know whether my recollections were such as to enable you to find the house."

Mease did, and one would think the mystery was solved. Yet at the Centennial Exposition of 1876, no historical markings appeared on the Graff House. Instead, the building next to it was labeled the "Jefferson House." That house was actually a former oyster house built in 1796, twenty years after the Declaration was written.

The misinformation was apparently deliberate and traceable to 1880, when a pair of rare book dealers known as the Jordan Brothers set up shop in the bogus building next door and issued business cards stating, "In this building, Thomas Jefferson wrote the Declaration of Independence."

In 1883, the correct building was scheduled for demolition to make room for a new bank. Shocked at the disregard for preserving history, Thomas Donaldson, a history buff, made plans to buy the doors, windows, frames, and other key components so as to rebuild the Graff House elsewhere. Before he could get to the materials, though, the destruction had begun. Donaldson removed what he could and planned to rebuild the Graff House in Washington, D.C. Those plans fell apart, though, when Dr. Spencer F. Baird, secretary of the Smithsonian Institution and a prime supporter of the project, died in 1888.

Making a nod to the historical importance of the location, a memorial plaque was put on the new Penn National Bank building. But once again, accuracy was eluded. Only half the plaque was in the right space. The other half ended up in front of what had been the bogus "Jefferson House." ✸

46

The Goodyear Bust
1826

Charles Goodyear, from New Haven, Connecticut, came to Philadelphia to apprentice in a hardware store when he was seventeen years old. He came back at twenty-six to open his own store.

But business didn't go so well for the man who would eventually become the father of the rubber industry in America and have blimps named after him.

His business in Philadelphia quickly went bankrupt and he spent time in debtor's prison, where he reportedly carried out his first rubber experiments. 🦋

The Chessmaster

1826

To all eyes, it looked like a mannequin of a Turkish gentleman sitting at a desk in front of a chessboard. When the desk drawer in the front was opened, audiences would see the mechanical inner workings of this, the famed Maelzel's Automaton, a chess-playing machine, which first visited Philadelphia in 1826.

Constructed in 1769 by a Hungarian nobleman, it was exhibited all over Europe, first arriving in Paris in 1783, moving afterward to London. When Baron von Kemplelen, the owner, died, it was sold to J. N. Maelzel, a musician and inventor from Bavaria who had, in 1815, invented the metronome and something called an automaton trumpeter.

But there was more to Maelzel's Automaton than the eye could see.

Curious paying audiences would see the Turk wheeled into a room. After the inner workings of the cabinet were shown (as well as openings on the Turk mannequin himself) to quell doubt from the crowd, the chess pieces would be

Joseph Jackson, *Encyclopedia of Philadelphia* (Harrisburg, Pa.: Harrisburg National Historical Association, 1932), pp. 858–859. Henry Ridgely Evans, *The Old and the New Magic* (1909), pp. 107–113.

put on the table. A large key was used to wind the automaton. A small chess board, set up at a separate table, would be provided for a challenger from the audience.

The automaton always chose white and made the first move, picking up a piece in its left hand and placing it in the desired square. Maelzel would then make the same move on the challenger's board and, likewise recreate the challenger's move on the automaton's board. The game continued until one player, usually the automaton, emerged victorious.

Not all spectators bought the claims of Maelzel. Early on, there were skeptics, among them a young Edgar Allen Poe, who noted:

> There is a man, Schlumberger, who attends him [Maelzel] wherever he goes, but who has no ostensible occupation other than that of assisting in packing and unpacking of the automaton. It is quite certain that he is never seen during the exhibition of the Chess Player, although frequently visible just before and after the exhibition. Moreover, some years ago, Maelzel visited Richmond with his automaton. Schlumberger was suddenly taken ill, and during his illness there was no exhibition of the Chess Player. . . . The inferences from all this we leave, without further comment, to the reader.

Such exposés made audiences more cynical and the Turk less popular on future visits.

Its tour was cut short, though, by an ill-fated trip to Cuba, on which both Schlumberger and Maelzel died of yellow fever. The Turk was stored in a Lombard Street warehouse and then sold at auction to pay off Maelzel's debts.

Magician Signor Blitz, a friend of the inventor, revealed the truth about the Turk after its master's death. Blitz wrote:

> The Chess Player was ingeniously constructed, a perfect counterpart of a magician's trick-table with a variety of partitions and doors, which, while they removed every possible appearance of deception, only produced greater mystery, and provided more security to the invisible player. The drawers and closets were so arranged as to enable him to change his position according to circumstances: at one moment he would be in this compartment; the next in that; then in the body of the Turk.

An intimate of Maelzel's, a Professor Allen, told of how the Turk would lose his chess matches when Schlumberger drank too much.

> On one occasion, just as Maelzel was bringing the Turk out from behind the curtain, a strange noise was heard . . . something between a rattle, a cough, and a sneeze. Maelzel pushed back his ally in evident alarm, but presently brought him forward again, and went on with the exhibition as if nothing had happened.

The Turk was bought by a group that included Poe's physician, Dr. John Kearsley, who exhibited it at the Franklin Institute (at its former location in what is now the Atwater Kent Museum) and at the Chinese Museum on Ninth Street. It was destroyed, along with the rest of the museum, in an 1854 fire. ✄

Gondar the Rhinoceros
1830

An ad appeared in Poulsen's *American Daily Advertiser* announcing that "The Wonder of the Animal Creation" would make an appearance at No. 48 South Fifth Street. No, it wasn't another elephant (see "A Mammoth Theater War"). Those were passé by the time this beast came to town.

This time, the big attraction was a 1,590-pound rhinoceros named Gondar, who was being exhibited in a room that had recently housed Maelzel's Automaton (see "The Chessmaster"). The rhino belonged to the King of Bisnee in Coos Beyhar, but an enterprising researcher named Dr. M. Burrough brought him to the United States for display.

The lengthy ad went on:

> Though stupid and savage by nature the Rhinoceros is not altogether incapable of domestication or insensible to the kindlier affections, as is evinced in the habits of the present specimen, which is perfectly

Advertisements in *Poulson's American Daily Advertiser*. January 1–31, 1831.

gentle, and obedient to the commands of his keeper (who is a native of Bengal).

The Apartment in which the above animal is placed, is always kept in the most cleanly order, and Females need entertain no compunction or delicacy of feeling in accompanying their Husbands or friends to visit it.

Apparently, though, things didn't go well for the rhino. In January of the following year, another ad appeared in the same newspaper bearing the headline: "Positive Sale. A Rhinoceros at Public Auction."

Still housed at No. 48 South Fifth Street, the beast was on the block "owing to the decease of one of the Company who lately purchased at private sale the Rhinoceros." Apparently the sale went well, since later in the month, the Walnut Street Theatre announced that, along with a musical parody of *Faustus* called *Dr. Foster; or Life in Philadelphia* and Mr. Asten's "pleasing feats of horsemanship," another act will be on the bill: "the Rhinoceros will be introduced in the ring." ✳

Brother Bonaparte
1841

In 1806 he became the king of Naples. Two years later, under orders from his brother, he led the French armies into Spain. In 1815, the French were defeated at Waterloo.

So what was Joseph Bonaparte to do while his kid brother, Napoleon, retired to St. Helena? Move to New Jersey, of course.

But first he tried New York. He arrived August 19, 1817, and took a room in a boardinghouse under the alias M. Bouchard. After being recognized on the street, he fled to the home of Commodore Lewis in New Jersey. The two journeyed to Washington but were headed off by a representative of the Navy Office.

Philadelphia was more hospitable. Here Kentucky congressman Henry Clay offered his personal suite at the Madison House Hotel while Bonaparte looked for a place to settle. But first things first: he needed to find a mistress. He met Annette Savage, a Quaker, put her up in a house south of the city, and then found himself a suitable home. For $17,500, he purchased Point Breeze, a three-story mansion near Bordentown, New Jersey.

Hundreds of crates filled with furnishings and paintings (including works by da Vinci and Rubens) were shipped to the estate, and an artificial lake was built and populated with swans. Instead of bringing his mistress with him, Bonaparte sent her to the home of a friend. There she bore two children, one of whom was killed when struck by a falling flowerpot.

That may have been the strangest, but it wasn't the family's last tragedy. While he was in Trenton in 1820, a fire rumored to be started by a local Russian diplomat destroyed the estate. After hearing how Bordentown residents rushed to save most of his artwork from the flames, Bonaparte commented in an oft-reprinted letter: "The Americans are, without contradiction, the best people I have ever known."

Ten years later, Napoleon II died, leaving Joseph, then sixty-four, next in line for the throne if the family ever returned to power. Joseph did not relish the possibility. In April 1841, after a massive stroke, he returned to Naples and spent the last three years of his life with his wife, Queen Julie, whom he had not seen in twenty-five years. 🦋

Samuel Scott's Last Leap

1841

This unfortunate man had announced his usual diving feats from Waterloo Bridge this forenoon, and consequently a great crowd collected to witness them. After performing several of his usual tricks, which he did successfully, and while going through the operation of hanging by his feet and neck alternately, it appears that the noose slipped.

And so began a notice of the last performance of Philadelphia daredevil Samuel Gilbert Scott, a would-be nineteenth-century Houdini.

Scott's diving abilities first attracted attention while he was with the U.S. Navy, where, for the amusement of himself and others, he leaped from the top masts of ships. Few would have suspected that he would turn this habit into a career.

Ricky Jay, *Learned Men and Fireproof Women*. New York: Villard Books, 1987 pp. 149–154.

According to magician/historian Ricky Jay, a chronicler of unusual entertainers, Scott toured the East Coast after leaving the navy, leaping from whatever structure happened to be over water, including a very dangerous Niagara Falls jump that killed another daredevil years later. Scott would pass the hat at the end of each dive and, in this manner, earned enough of a reputation and a bankroll to journey to Europe.

In 1840, he arrived in England and proceeded to leap off everything from a one hundred forty-foot scaffold at Brighton Pier to a forty-foot cliff at Cornwall.

On January 11, 1841, Scott planned an especially unusual stunt. He would run from a pub in Drury Lane to Waterloo Bridge, take a forty-foot leap into the river, and return to his spot at the bar within an hour. Not only that, once he reached the top of the diving platform, he would perform acrobatic maneuvers with a noose around his neck, something he had done before in other locations.

This time, though, the noose slipped. Spectators watched as Scott spent minutes dangling in front of them. One member of the audience, a little more perceptive than the rest, finally climbed the scaffold and cut Scott down.

"A surgeon was immediately sent for," the notice continued, "and an attempt was made to bleed the unfortunate man, but without success."

Building a Better Dinosaur

1841

During the first half of the 1800s, digging up bones in America was all the rage. With so much unexplored territory and so many previously uncatalogued creatures, fossil finders were having a field day.

Among them was Dr. Albert Koch, a German-born immigrant based in St. Louis who explored the southern states looking for bones. These he would arrange into exhibits for the public, then, when interest waned, sell them to museums eager for interesting displays.

One of his most notorious discoveries was what he claimed was a ten-thousand-year-old mastodon in Benton County, Missouri, the bones of which he had found under layers of clay, gravel, and quicksand.

He called it Missourium and took it on a tour of America, arriving in Philadelphia at the Masonic Hall in 1841. It did not take long for the American Philosophical

Robert Silverberg, *Scientists and Scoundrels* (New York: Thomas Y. Crowell, 1965), pp. 51–70.

57

Society, the scientific association founded by Benjamin Franklin, to hear about the beast on display in town.

A Koch enthusiast, Dr. Richard Harlan, addressed the society in praise of Koch's discoveries, although he did note that the assembly of the bones was, to put it mildly, creative. Specifically, Koch had turned the curved tusks into horns and placed them on top of the beast's head. Also, Koch didn't let the fact that more than one set of bones were found at the site get in the way of his assemblage. Instead of sorting them out, he added all the bones together to create a single jumbo mastodon.

These obvious scientific flubs, according to Harlan, were no reason to dismiss Koch. "No doubt," noted Harlan, Koch soon would "rectify these errors." Wishful thinking.

The enthusiasm of Koch and the society led Koch to other reconstructions, including a 114-foot-long, 7,500-pound sea monster which he displayed four years later in New York. At first he called the beast Hydrarchus sillimani, but after a critic said, "It would be a silly man indeed who believed in Hydrarchus sillimani," Koch changed its name to Hydrarchus harlani, in honor of his Philadelphia apologist Dr. Richard Harlan, who couldn't rethink his opinion of Koch since Harlan had died in 1843. ✳

A Shot at Scott
1843

In 1838, the Pennsylvania constitution granted the right to vote to all white male citizens over the age of twenty-one. One of the first men to benefit from this was John Morin Scott, a New York–born Princeton graduate, who defeated Samuel Badger to become the first mayor of Philadelphia to be chosen by direct vote and not by appointment by an elected city council.

But not everyone was happy with the new mayor, especially not Adalberte Benedictus Ptolemeis. On May 3, 1843, Ptolemeis walked into the mayor's office and demanded a job teaching Italian and geometry. He also presented Scott with a paper written entirely in French.

The Mayor wasn't sure how to handle the visitor. He first tried offering the odd guy in the dark cloak some money, but Ptolemeis refused.

Next he tried getting up to leave the office, but Ptolemeis took a pistol out from under his cloak and shot the mayor in the back. The bullet went through the mayor's coat and his vest, but was stopped by his silk suspenders.

It would not be the last projectile that struck Scott (see "The Protestant/Catholic Riots"), but the oft-targeted mayor continued to serve as the city's mayor for three terms, until 1844.

The Protestant/
Catholic Riots
1844

Tension were high in the early 1840s between Protestant residents and newly arrived Irish Catholic immigrants. Among other things, the Catholics resented the use of the King James version of the Bible in public schools; the Protestants complained about foreigners thinking they could change the established order.

Calling themselves Native Americans, a group of Protestants began to show their numbers in public meetings. This led Alderman Hugh Clark, a devout Catholic, to introduce legislation banning Bible readings altogether in public schools.

In protest, Protestants took to the streets of Kensington. At the time, Kensington had one of the largest Irish-Catholic pockets in the area. Residents there reacted to the gathering by rushing the speakers' platform, destroying it, and bombarding the Protestants with various objects.

The following Monday, the determined Protestants returned to the same location. This time, in the midst of a rainstorm, a shot rang out; one of their number dropped. They reacted by pelting local homes with rocks.

Both sides eventually faced off with pistols and stones across the market at Germantown Road and Master Street, each taking turns advancing and retreating to resupply. The battle continued into the night and included the destruction of the Female Roman Catholic Seminary at Second and Phoenix streets.

The next day, a Protestant meeting at Independence Square was followed by a march up to battle-weary Kensington. Another shot was fired, by whom it is not known, and another battle raged. Included among the combatants this time was a group of Irish rooftop snipers. The Protestants fought fire with fire by torching the houses under the snipers' feet. In the process, they set fire to thirty buildings in the area.

Mayor John Morin Scott attempted to stand in the way of the mob, which was on its way to attack St. Augustine's Church at 4th and Vine. He was quickly felled by a well-thrown rock.

Sporadic fighting continued, climaxing in a four-day battle in Southwark. The fighting ended only when five thousand members of the state militia were called in. By that time, two more churches had been destroyed, along with Alderman Clark's home. ✺

The End of the World,

PART 2

1844

They were called Millerites. And they believed what Vermont farmer William Miller told them—that the second coming of Christ was at hand wherein the living would head for heaven and the dead would rise to face judgment.

Miller's calculations showed that the event would occur "sometime between March 21, 1843, and March 21, 1844." After nothing happened, he moved up the date to October 23, 1844. On October 22, 1844, a group of Philadelphians left their church at Vine and Juliana streets and gathered in Isaac Yocoomb's field in Darby, Pennsylvania.

The crowd of believers were so confident that worldly

David Armstrong and Elizabeth Metzger Armstrong, *The Great American Medicine Show: Being an Illustrated History of Hucksters, Healers, Health Evangelists, and Heroes from Plymouth Rock to the Present* (Englewood Cliffs, N.J., 1991), p. 100. Joseph Jackson, *Encyclopedia of Philadelphia* (Harrisburg, Pa.: Harrisburg National Historical Association, 1932), pp. 890–891. J. Thomas Scharf and Thompson Westcott, *History of Philadelphia 1609–1884* (Philadelphia: L. H. Everts, 1884), p. 675.

goods could be left behind that many left their houses and businesses unlocked. "This shop is closed in honor of the King of Kings," read one sign, "who will appear about the 20th of October. Get ready, friends, to crown Him Lord of all!"

The "last day" attracted crowds of gawkers who watched the believers, wearing "ascension robes," praying and waiting for the end of the world. One man waited by his wife's grave ready to catch her when she took off for heaven.

It didn't happen. But it did rain.

The next day, definitely the last "last day" according to believers, another tent was raised to handle the crowd. Tears fell and prayers went up as the crowd awaited midnight.

Again, nothing.

Some waited through the twenty-fourth. The rest, soggy and cold, went home. ➤✖

Prayers upon the Water

1847

They that go down to the sea in ships, that do business in great waters. These see the works of the Lord, and his wonders in the deep.

—Psalms 107: 23–31

Inspired by those words, the Churchmen's Missionary Association for Seamen of the port of Philadelphia was founded in 1847 to enhance the spiritual life of the watered class.

The goal was lofty. According to Joseph Eves Hover, in his essay "Commerce With the Position of the Sailor

J. Thomas Scharf and Thompson Westcott, *History of Philadelphia 1609–1884* (Philadelphia: L. H. Everts, 1884), p. 1362. Joseph Eves Hover, "An Essay on Commerce, with the Position of the Sailor Therewith" (Philadelphia: Women's Auxiliary of the Association for Seamen, 1890). Rev. Washington B. Erden, *The Churchmen's Missionary Association for Seamen of the Port of Philadelphia* (Philadelphia: Association for Seamen, 1875). Joseph Jackson, *Encyclopedia of Philadelphia* (Harrisburg, Pa.: Harrisburg National Historical Association, 1932), p. 668.

Therewith," "The common sailor has no provisions made for his temporal or spiritual welfare. . . . He must be guarded against the tempter in the guise of some professed friend by whom he is only led to sin and ruin."

The long-term goals weren't just for the comfort of the sailors, however. The essay went on:

> It is by such means as above narrated that those men of the sea may be made the lay missionaries to the desolate people of the earth, who know not the Gospel of Jesus Christ. And when the common sailors shall be thus engaged, then will be fulfilled the prophecy, "That the waste and desolate places of the earth shall blossom as the rose, and joy and peace shall dwell therein."

One unique plan to save the souls of sailors was the Church of the Redeemer, which was moored at Dock Street beginning in 1847—moored because Redeemer was a floating church. Believed to have been the first of its kind in the country, it lasted on the Philadelphia side of the river until 1851, when the pier it was connected to was leased for commercial purposes. Without a Philadelphia berth, the church was towed to Camden, where it housed a small congregation until one Christmas morning when it was destroyed in a fire. ✄

Dueling Shakespeares

1849

"So foul and fair a day I have not seen." In character as Macbeth, noted British thespian William Charles Macready spoke these words from the stage of the Astor Place Opera House in New York. Macbeth was foreshadowing the play's upcoming murders, but the actor may well have had another horror on his mind. Outside, a crowd had gathered, convinced that Macready had insulted Philadelphia's foremost man of the stage—Edwin Forrest.

At fourteen, Forrest had made his debut at the Walnut Street Theatre. By 1827, he was a twenty-two-year-old star.

Fame in America wasn't enough. Forrest wanted his talents praised in the birthplace of Shakespeare. So, in 1845, he launched a tour of Britain. Expecting praise, Forrest was shocked when London audiences hissed at his Hamlet and the press backed up their opinion. Forrest was convinced that local acting favorite William Macready, with whom he had dined during the tour, was secretly behind the insults.

To retaliate, Forrest traveled to Edinburgh and took a box seat at Macready's *Hamlet*. The American star then loudly hissed during the prince's madness scene.

Scandal erupted. Letters and editorials hit the papers. Tensions continued to build until 1849, when Macready came to New York to perform at Astor Place. His first performance went badly, with audience members—without the help of Forrest—howling. Embarrassed New York aristocrats talked Macready into performing again two days later, the same night that Forrest was in town in another theater performing the part of Spartacus in *The Gladiator*.

Pro-Forrest "Bowery B'hoys" blanketed the city with leaflets encouraging all proud Americans to meet for Macready's performance. They did—somewhere between 10,000 and 24,000, along with 325 police officers, eight companies of National Guardsmen, a troop of light artillery, and two troops of cavalry.

Inside the theater, the Macready fans outnumbered the Forresters 9 to 1. Despite a ten-minute curtain delay, the first two scenes of *Macbeth* went well. Until Macready walked on stage, that is. Then the hissing began. But that was nothing compared with the behavior outside the theater, where, as the second act began, the crowd threw stones and bricks at the theater.

The police swung their clubs and sprayed the crowd with water, but this failed to subdue the mob. So the militia was called in. After Macready took his final bow, the order to fire was given. In the resulting battle, 31 people were killed, 150 wounded, and 86 arrested.

Macready never again performed in the United States. ✄

Poe Undercover

1849

r. Sartain, I have come to you for a refuge and protection. . . . Will you let me stay with you? It is necessary for my safety that I lie concealed for a time."

Both John Sartain and the haggard visitor at his door were known to the Philadelphia literary community. Sartain was a publisher of some renown as well as an illustrator and engraver. The visitor, Edgar Allan Poe, had long established a reputation for unusual writing—and equally unusual behavior.

On this occasion, in 1849, Poe informed Sartain that while on his way by train to New York he had heard some men sitting a few seats away plotting to kill him and throw his body off. It was only Poe's acute hearing that saved him. When the train stopped at Bordentown, New Jersey, Poe quietly got off and caught the next one back to Philadelphia.

Sartain's belief that this was all a creation of Poe's paranoid imagination did little to calm the would-be target. "If this mustache of mine were removed," Poe suggested, "I should not be so readily recognized. Will you lend me a razor, that I may shave it off?" Not being a shaver, Sartain had none to offer. Instead, he performed the operation using scissors, hoping that things would appear more sensible to Poe in the morning.

The night was still young, however. After tea, Sartain noticed Poe preparing to go out and asked about his destination. "To the Schuylkill," Poe announced. Sartain volunteered to go along, even supplying slippers to replace Poe's worn shoes.

The pair hopped an omnibus at Ninth and Chestnut and got off at the river near Callowhill. There they climbed to the top of the bridge. While up on the bridge, Poe, in a confessional mood, revealed that he had once been thrown into Moyamensing Prison for counterfeiting. While in jail, Poe claimed, he saw a woman standing on the battlements of the prison. "She addressed to me a series of questions," Poe recounted. "Had I failed once either to hear or to make pertinent answer, the consequences to me would have been fearful." Once again, he said, his acute hearing saved his life.

According to Poe, an attendant then asked him if he would like to take a walk and see something interesting, which turned out to be nothing but a kettle of boiling spirits. The attendant asked if he would like to take a drink but Poe refused. Then Poe's mother-in-law, Mrs. Clemm, appeared, and the attendants proceeded to saw off first her feet, then her calves.

Alarmed at Poe's story, Sartain took Poe back to his house and put his friend to bed. Sartain later learned that Poe had been in Moyamensing Prison, though not on counterfeiting charges. He was jailed for drunkenness.

69

Two days later, Poe arose and claimed to feel much better. After a long walk and a period of rest face down in the grass, he confessed to Sartain that the whole assassination plot he had heard on the train was a delusion. With that, Poe borrowed money from his host and took off for New York, never to see Sartain or Philadelphia again.

Ever Heard of
Carl Rumpp?
1850

German immigrant Carl Frederich Rumpp opened his first leather-making shop at Fourth and Arch streets in 1850. From there, until 1964, he and his successors at the Rumpp Company produced ladies' change purses, cigar cases, memo books, Union Army cartridge belts, and the first American billfolds.

During World War I, a California entrepreneur decided to try raising a herd of ostriches, which are usually found in South Africa. Wartime supplies were scarce, and the businessman could not feed the beasts, opting instead to kill two hundred of them. But what to do with the hides? He asked around among acquaintances and discovered that Rumpp's was the place to go. He shipped samples to Philadelphia. The two hundred ostrich martyrs were turned into purses, key cases, and game sets, making Rumpp the first manufacturer of ostrich skin accessories in the world.

Rumpp took advantage of another animal tragedy in

G. Don Fairbairn, *Philadelphia: The Fabulous City of Firsts*, (Wyncote, Pa.: Kirsh Publishing, 1976), p. 39.

71

the name of fashion when eleven performing elephants from Ringling Brothers Circus were killed in an accident. A bidding war took off quickly for the exotic skins. Rumpp won and the pachyderms became billfolds, stud boxes, tobacco pouches, and collar cases. ✼

The Caveman, PART 2
1856

The story of Albert Large would not seem out of place in a collection of fairy tales alongside Hansel and Gretel. Born in 1805, Large was always in trouble. Instead of going to school, he would wander off into the woods of Bucks County. A favorite hideaway was a place called Wolf's Rock, where she-wolves were known to have their litters.

After Large's mother died, his stepmother had no better luck in keeping the boy under control. Large didn't leave home, though, until he was in his thirties. It was a crush he had on a girl living nearby that finally got him to leave home. The girl kept rejecting his advances and, when Large finally got the hint, he decided to relocate to Wolf's Rock and set up house in a cave.

To keep the wolves out in daytime, Large would cover the opening with a rock and go about his business, which often included stealing from the houses within walking distance. He stayed there for more than twenty years, avoiding his family, who continued searching for the missing man.

Carl Sifakis, *Great American Eccentrics: Strange and Peculiar People* (New York: Galahad Books, 1984), pp. 83–84.

On April 9, 1858, hunters stumbled upon Large's cave. For a brief while, he became something of a folk hero among the locals, but Large disappeared again into the woods, never to be heard from again. ✸

A New Chief in Town,

PART 1

1856

Barbarous gangs with names like "Rats," "Stingers," "Buffers," "Skinners," and, of all things, "Gumballs," roamed the streets of Philadelphia for years. But none caused more trouble than the "Schuylkill Rangers," who claimed the corner of Twenty-third and Market as their turf. They were, according to one contemporary, experts at "highway robbery and looting of vessels, dwellings and stores."

Street crime came from other sources, too. Rival companies of volunteer firemen fought in the streets, setting their own fires and stealing whatever they could get their hands on as they pretended to fight the blaze.

It looked like Philadelphia needed a top law-and-order person. Somebody like Richard Vaux.

Vaux's background was unusual. At 20, he was admitted to the Pennsylvania bar. Then a twist of fate during a European visit led him to accept the position of secretary of the American legation at the Court of St. James. A year later,

Benjamin Rush arrived from the United States and allowed
Vaux to finish his trip.

Returning to London, he found himself in the company of royalty. When word reached Philadelphia papers
that he had been dancing with Queen Victoria, his Quaker
mother commented, "I do hope Richard will not marry out
of meeting."

Mother Vaux had nothing to fear. Soon her son returned to Philadelphia and displayed remarkable tenacity.
After four unsuccessful bids for mayor, he finally, at age
forty, led the Democrats to victory in the biennial election of
1856.

Safety in the streets was priority one. After his inaugu-
ration, Vaux drafted his own set of rules for the police department. He enlarged the force to one thousand men and
formed a reserve corps composed of sixty of Philadelphia's
finest who would always be on call, and housed them at
Fifth and Chestnut. Vaux also appointed two fire detectives
to deal with the rowdy volunteers.

To fight the Schuylkill Rangers, Vaux stationed another sixty men along the river from Fairmount to the Navy
Yard. By his own admission, they made no formal arrests.
Instead, he allowed his men to administer justice that was a
little less subtle. Said Vaux:

> The fellow who was caught never forgot until his
> dying day the time he fell into the hands of Dick
> Vaux's police. I remember one night three of the
> Rangers were surprised, and jumped into the river
> and swam to a tugboat. . . . It was very cold and they

76

thought [we] would not follow. They were never so
much mistaken in all their lives.

The erstwhile mayor would often go along with the police
on such patrols. And he got results. Physical assaults (at
least by criminals) declined and no major riots occurred
under Vaux's watch.

In 1858, Vaux was defeated in his fifth mayoral bid by
Alexander Henry and the People's Party. Undaunted, Vaux
ran for and won a congressional seat in 1890. He completed
his more than fifty years of public service in 1892 as inspec-
tor of the Eastern State Penitentiary, where, undoubtedly,
he ran into some old acquaintances.   🦋

"Have Mercy, God!
The Trains Have Met!"
1856

The North Pennsylvania Railroad had a rule back in the 1850s. It was a very simple rule that was in place for what proved to be a very good reason. Any southbound train arriving at Fort Washington had to wait around for an excursion special to cruise past. If none came by within fifteen minutes, the engineer was to proceed slowly and send a horse and rider ahead to let the late excursion train know that there was another train on the track.

"Frightful Loss of Life," "Appalling Disaster," and "Latest from the Scene of the Accident," *Philadelphia Evening Bulletin*, July 17, 1856. "Relief for the Sufferers," and "The Terrible Railroad Disaster." *Philadelphia Evening Bulletin*, July 18, 1856. "The Railroad Tragedy," *Philadelphia Evening Bulletin*, July 19, 1856. "The Railroad Disaster," *Philadelphia Evening Bulletin*, July 21, 1856. "Railroad Calamity," *Philadelphia Evening Bulletin*, July 25, 1856. Freeman H. Hubbgard, "Railroaders" in George Korson, ed. *Pennsylvania Songs and Legends* (Philadelphia: University of Pennsylvania Press, 1949), pp. 311–312. Norm Cohen, *Long Steel Rail: The Railroad in American Folksong* (Urbana: University of Illinois Press, 1981), pp. 175–177.

On July 17, 1856, William S. Lee decided to disregard that rule, which resulted in a collision and fire that cost sixty-six lives. Lee, a dentist by profession but on this day the engineer of the southbound train, proved vague in the latter investigation about such key issues as the time he left Fort Washington. He also admitted that he didn't send a rider ahead to warn any northbound trains. The other train's conductor, fearing blame for the accident, poisoned himself.

The incident inspired the first American song commemorating a train wreck, titled "The Killed by the Accident on the North Pennsylvania Railroad, July 17th 1856." Some lyrics include:

> When they were in the burning cars, in sorrow and
> in fright,
> With aching hearts and willing hands they worked
> with all their might;
> But O! their time it was too short, their fatal hour
> had come,
> For God their King knew all things best, and took
> them to their home.

The song was followed shortly after by another ballad, "Verses on the Death of Miss Annie Lilly."

> But oh! what means this sudden jar:
> This wild confusion in the cars,
> These shrieks that now assail the ear,
> And fill the stoutest hearts with fear!
> What flames are those, the now arise!

What horrid screams, and awful cries!
Those dying prayers, I'll ne'er forget,

Noble efforts, both, but according to Norm Cohen, author of *Long Steel Rail: The Railroad in American Folksong*, "Neither ballad seems to have left any mark on oral tradition."

Even without a memorable ballad, the wreck did leave its mark on history. Among those who rushed to the sight was Mary Benjamin Ambler, who brought first-aid supplies. Her assistance in taking care of the victims led the railroad company to name the station after her. The town that grew around the station became known, also, as Ambler.

Killing Catto

1871

Octavius B. Catto was one hell of a baseball player. He had learned cricket while at the Institute for Colored Youth (later Cheyney State College) and afterward picked up the American version of the game, which was gaining in popularity.

Catto became captain of the Pythians, the second black baseball team in Philadelphia (after the Excelsiors). Competition was tough, leading to many family feuds over divided loyalties between the two teams.

The first black team to visit the city, the Bachelors of

"Record of Matches—Games Played during the Season Just Closed," November 4, 1868. From the collection of the Historical Society of Pennsylvania. "Voting and Rioting," *Philadelphia Inquirer*, October 11, 1871. "Retribution's Reckoning," *Philadelphia Press*, April 24, 1877. "The Prisoner Is the Man," *Philadelphia Press*, April 25, 1877. "Not Guilty!" *Philadelphia Press*, May 5, 1877. Harry C. Silcox, "In Memory of Marcus A. Foster, 1923–1973," *Harvard Educational Review*, February 1974, pp. 1–5. Harry C. Silcox, "Nineteenth-Century Black Militant: Octavius V. Catto, 1839–1871," *Pennsylvania Magazine of History*, January 1977. *The Trial of Frank Kelly for the Assassination and Murder of Octavius v. Catto*, compiled by Henry H. Griffin (Philadelphia (OK?): Daily Tribune Publishing, 1871) pp. 43–44. "Pencil Pusher Points," *Philadelphia Tribune*, August 24, 1912.

Albany, came to play the Pythians in 1867. By the end of 1867, the Pythians had an outstanding record of 9 and 1. Still wanting to improve the team, Catto and his teammates strategized that they needed more spring practice and some new blood. They picked up two new players, who helped carry them to an undefeated season in 1867. Scorecard records tell of five-inning games reaching scores of 73 to 142. It was a hitter's game.

The Pythians' popularity, and Catto's fame, grew.

But this was more than baseball. Visiting other cities, and having other ball clubs come to Philadelphia, was occasion for parties, dances and, most disturbing to the white power structure, open discussions about the injustices of the day.

The next year, the Convention of Baseball Clubs was formed in Harrisburg. The Pythians attempted to join the league, but were turned down.

Catto's career was cut short in 1869. That year, Pennsylvania ratified the Fifteenth Amendment, which allowed blacks to vote. Federal troops were sent to Philadelphia to protect that right.

Troops from the First Division were ordered to their armories to await orders. For Catto, that meant the Colored Brigade at 505 Chestnut Street. He reported there and then headed home to don his uniform and arm himself. At South Street, near Ninth, he ran into a gang of white men with guns. Catto was shot several times before falling dead into the arms of two policemen. Constable Barr pursued the killer, Frank Kelly, to a taproom at Ninth and Bainbridge, arrested him, and turned him over to the police, from whom he escaped.

The Philadelphia black community was furious. A meeting was held at the National Guards' Hall and a resolution passed denouncing the police. A reward was offered for the capture of the murderer.

Kelly, a bartender with a long record of altercations with the law, had been treated that morning at Pennsylvania Hospital for a wound earned in a fight with a black man.

Foreshadowing what would happen after the assassination of Martin Luther King, Jr. almost a century later, newspaperman Henry Griffin of the *Daily Tribune* noted:

> All sorts of rumors were prevalent after the decease of . . . Catto, about his past life and his great love for women. . . . That letters were found in his trunk, showing that he was engaged to three or more of the opposite sex, and that he was seen to frequent a certain Ice Cream Saloon with one of the fair ones, and that Frank Kelly was snubbed by her on account of Catto's flirtations with her, is another one of the many rumors, all of which perhaps have not the least foundation. At any rate, there was no plausible reason to so suddenly dispatch this promising young man into eternity. 🦋

The Epizooty
1872

In 1872, the "epizooty" struck Philadelphia. That's what the locals called an epidemic of "epizootic distemper" that plagued the city's animals for about a month.

The disease did not only affect pet owners and zookeepers, however. It also crippled the city's transportation system. Without horses to power their systems, two railway lines cut back to one day a week, some cut back on Sunday service, and the delivery of goods and services was nearly stopped, except for enterprising and strong backed businesspeople who decided to draw their carts themselves.

Reese D. James, *Old Drury of Philadelphia* (New York: Greenwood Press, 1968), p. 838.

The Great Keely Motor Hoax

1872

Will you please take the time and trouble to let me know how the motor is coming on. I have three shares of the full paid capital stock of the Keely Motor Company. I am a poor woman . . . and trying to support an old mother, eighty-four years of age, by taking Summer boarders . . . I have faith in the motor and hope you can write me some encouraging news.

Joseph Bulgatz, *Ponzi Schemes, Invaders from Mars and More Extraordinary Popular Delusions and the Madness of Crowds* (New York: Harmony Books, 1992), pp. 317–321. "Keely, The Inventor, Dead," *New York Times*, November 19, 1898. "Keely's Motor in Boston," *New York Times*, January 4, 1899. "Keely's Personal Estate," *New York Times*, January 5, 1899. "Mrs. Bloomfield Moore Dead," *New York Times*, January 6, 1899. "Keely Secrets Laid Bare," *Philadelphia Press*, January 16, 1899. "Keely's Secret Disclosed," *New York Times*, January 20, 1899. "Keely's Odd Tubes and Shere," *Philadelphia Press*, January 20, 1899. "The Keely Expose Discussed," *Philadelphia Press*, January 21, 1899.

So read one of the many letters found in the home of John W. Keely after his death in 1898.

Had the Keely Motor Company been all that Keely said it was, his investors would have become millionaires and his name would now be mentioned with Franklin and Edison. It wasn't. And his name comes up only when massive hoaxes are recalled.

The smooth-talking Keely began his fundraising in 1872. He went on a lengthy lecture tour, telling anyone who would listen that all atoms were in constant vibration and that, with proper funding, he could make the atoms in a substance vibrate in unison. The resulting energy—he called it "etheric force"—could then be used to run a motor.

With funds in place, he set up the Keely Motor Company in New York and rapidly recruited investors with his talk of "etheric disintegration" and his "hydro-pneumatic, pulsatic vacuum engine." He boasted that he could create "a vapor of so fine an order it will penetrate metal" and claimed that he once drove an engine 800 RPMs using only a thimbleful of water.

Keely set up his laboratory in Philadelphia, on the 1400 block of North 20th Street. Within two years he announced that his invention was complete. He would now allow potential investors in for a demonstration, provided he had twenty-four hours' notice. Once the crowd was in his laboratory, Keely would blow a mouth organ and the onlookers would see a lever lifting a 550-pound weight. Why was this so astounding? Keely, at least in demonstrations before 1887, claimed that "vaproci tension" was moving the machine. After 1887, his story changed a bit, and he claimed that the force came by wire and was purely vibratory.

Some had their doubts about either story. The Wizard of Menlo Park himself, Thomas Edison, had asked to make a complete study of Keely's lab and was refused. Not a good sign in scientific circles.

But despite the skepticism among the scientific community, there were many believers. Keely once told a gentleman:

> You may not believe me, but what I say is true. In a short time I can come up here to his office, I can seat you and your whole office force upon that fireproof safe over there in the corner, and I can then cause the whole thing, with you on top, to sail out of the window. I can make the safe float around out there, and I can bring it back to its place again.

In 1881, Keely hit paydirt when he met Clara Jessup Bloomfield-Moore, a widow who had, just a year earlier, established the Bloomfield-Moore art collection in the Franklin Institute in honor of her late husband. With Keely's talk about being able to send a steamship from New York to Liverpool and back with a gallon of water, she quickly became convinced that the motor was legit, giving him $250 to $300 a month for his personal use.

Some of the stockholders were worried because Keely refused to take out patents, claiming that he would then have to reveal essential information about his invention. But Bloomfield-Moore was undaunted. A promoter as well as an investor, she once wrote of Keely's force as "like the sun behind the clouds, the source of all light though itself unseen."

An 1884 report in *Scientific American* claimed everything Keely asserted his machine could do could easily be replicated using compressed air. But the scam was not verified until after his death, when twenty large packing crates were shipped to Boston, where T.B. Kinraide, an inventor, accepted the shipment and added them to his own laboratory. "He never fully explained the secret of his perpetual motion to me," said Kinraide, "but I feel that I know more of the motor than any other man."

When Keely's workshop was dismantled, though, an investigation proved that Keely's motor was pure trickery. A team that included an engineer, a University of Pennsylvania assistant professor of physics, and an experimental psychology colleague, as well as an expert in mound digging, was sent in to investigate.

They discovered small brass tubes concealed in the brickwork under the floor of the lab. The tubing was connected to the steel sphere that Keely had insisted was generating energy without tubing.

In his report, Professor Hering, the consulting engineer, wrote:

> Personally I am satisfied now that he used highly compressed air, and that he intentionally and knowingly deceived the public when he held his exhibitions. Moreover, there is nothing wonderful about any of these experiments of which I have seen descriptions, if he used highly compressed air.

Among those who chimed in with a defense of Keely even after the evidence mounted was Nicola Tesla, of "Tesla coil" fame. Said Tesla:

"I have known for four years the so-called secret of inventor Keely, . . . I would like to believe that Keely was not a dishonest fellow. . . . Although he evidently used compressed air in his experiments, it does not follow that he did this to deliberately deceive." ✀

Alas, Poor Pop

1874

J ohn "Pop" Reed got his first job at the Walnut
Street Theatre in 1830 as a stagehand. His last job
at the theater was 111 years later, in 1941, when
he—or more correctly, part of him—appeared as a prop. Or
so the story goes.

The brilliant career of Pop Reed fits neatly into two
halves. The first was fairly conventional. He worked for
years as a stagehand and then became the theater's door-
man. As would anyone who spent that much time around
such renowned thespians, Reed harbored a secret desire to
mount the stage himself and become an actor. According to
a fellow stagehand, Reed never missed a performance in his
forty-four years of active duty. He also fathered thirteen
children, two of whom became relatively famous performers.

But Pop Reed still had not made it to the front of the
footlights when he died in 1874. To some, death might have
meant the end of theatrical ambitions—this being the era of
live theater.

But Reed's will was strong, and he was prepared. His
will included very explicit instructions:

> My head is to be separated from my body . . . the latter to be buried in a grave; the former, duly macerated and prepared, to be brought to the theater where I served all my life, and to be employed to represent the skull of Yorick . . . and to this end I bequeath my head.

Legend has it that the skull was indeed used for performances of *Hamlet*, and was kept at the Walnut for years. Until it vanished.

It remained missing until 1941 when Kay Land, appearing at the Walnut as Aunt Cora in *Life with Father*, decided to ask some questions. She found out that the skull was first put in possession of a prop man named Charley. After Charley died the skull was passed on to his son. Land followed the twisted route until she found herself in the Academy of Music, where head property master (no pun intended) James P. McNeill acknowledged that he had the skull.

Reed's cranium was carried over to the theater in a paper bag and given to the Walnut's eight-year-old property master, George William Thorpe. Later he said, "You know, stage people then took the work more seriously than they do now."

The skull vanished again shortly thereafter and has yet to be found. ✄

Puttin' on the Blitz
1877

For years, they knew him on Green Street as the magician who gave lessons from his home. But in 1877, the street and the city mourned the passing of Signor Blitz (see "The Chessmaster"), Philadelphia's most notable magician as well as a ventriloquist and bird trainer of some note.

A native of Moravia, Blitz was so popular at his peak, that thirteen different impostors were traveling through the United States using variations of his name, specifically:

Signor Blitz; Signor Blitz, Jr.; Signor Blitz, The Original; Signor Blitz's Son; Signor Blitz's Nephew; Signor Blitz, The Wonderful; Signor Blitz, The

Evans Dictionary of American Biography, vol. 1, (1909) p. 378. "Obituary: Signor Blitz," *Philadelphia Inquirer*, January 29, 1877. Joseph Jackson, *Encyclopedia of Philadelphia* (Harrisburg, Pa.: Harrisburg National Historical Association, 1932), pp. 299–301. Signor Blitz, *A History of Ventriloquism with Instructions and Anecdotes Combined, Being a Highly Diverting Combination of Eccentric and Amusing Anecdotes, Illustrating the Astonishing Effects Produced by the Remarkable Faculty of Ventriloquism as Practiced by Signor Blitz* (Philadelphia: privately published, 1856).

Great; Signor Blitz, The Unrivalled; Signor Blitz, The Mysterious; Signor Blitz, By Purchase; and Signor Blitz, The Great Original.

"I have been in constant receipt of bills of their contracting," said Blitz in his biography, "for, not content with taking my name, they have not even honor enough to pay their debts."

After retiring from the stage, Blitz gave lessons at his home on Green Street.

Ooops

1884

 letter appearing in an 1884 issue of the *Philadelphia Medical News* was signed by a doctor Egerton Y. Davis.

The subject, penis captivus.

According to Davis's account, a coachman and a married woman were sharing indiscretions in bed when the woman's husband arrived. Surprised, the two became, through a medical quirk, stuck together. Called to the scene, Dr. Davis had to use chloroform on the woman to relax her enough to release her lover.

It took eighty-seven years to determine that the story was a hoax. Drs. Sidney W. Bondurant and Stephen C. Cappanari, both of Vanderbilt University Hospital, studied the alleged case and discovered that the writer was actually a Canadian doctor, Sir William Osler, who used the pseudonym to embarrass a colleague who was on staff at the *Medical News*.

Jan Harold Brunvand, *The Choking Doberman and Other "New" Urban Legends* (New York: W. W. Norton, 1984), pp. 143–144.

The Duel

1879

It wasn't a love triangle or a financial dispute that led to the last recorded gentlemen's duel among Philadelphians. It was fashion criticism.

Dr. J. William "Bill" White was named surgeon to the First City Troop of the U.S. Cavalry in 1879. But what to wear when on duty? Tradition called for white trousers and a blue frock coat. But White, a graduate of Penn Medical School, just didn't think that outfit was him. So he asked permission simply to wear his old troop uniform.

Not everyone liked the idea, particularly one Robert Adams, Jr. Adams made disparaging remarks about the length of White's tails and these comments were relayed to White. At first, White chose to take the high road and ignore the man. But after others repeated the remarks, he felt he had to do something. He went with a friend to Adams's home and asked for an explanation.

White was given an unrecorded one that, whatever it was, apparently was not what he wanted to hear. He retaliated to the slander by decking Adams with a blow to the jaw. This did not sit well with Adams, who challenged White to a duel. Pistols were selected as the weapon and the two met on the Maryland/Delaware border. They walked their paces (accounts differ as to whether it was fifteen or thirty), turned, fired . . . and missed. (According to witnesses, White fired into the air.) The two then shook hands and went about their business.

The story made the newspapers, where editorials railed against the reckless action and foolish argument. But the incident did not get in the way of either of their careers.

Adams went on to be United States Minister to Brazil.

White went on to become the first director of Physical Education at the University of Pennsylvania. He also was appointed by President McKinley in 1899 to be a member of the Board of Visitors of the Annapolis Naval Academy. There, he performed the one act whose repercussions were felt well past his days—he was instrumental in helping to persuade Navy's football team to play Army's at Philadelphia's Franklin Field.

White also had further temper trouble. He once pulled his carriage over when a pedestrian swore at him. When the apology he demanded was not given, he struck the man. This time no shots were fired. ✌

No Accounting for Taste
1880

R udyard Kipling, upon hearing publisher Edward Box talk of Philadelphia scrapple, asked his Delaware Valley friend to send him a sample. Bok shipped him several pounds of the substance and Kipling, author of *The Jungle Book* and "Gunga Din," expressed his gratitude in a letter.

> By the way, that scrapple—which by token is a dish for the Gods—arrived in perfect condition, and I ate it all, or as much as I could get hold of. I am extremely grateful for it. It's all nonsense about pig being unwholesome. There isn't a Mary-ache in a barrel of scrapple.

Later in the letter, though, Kipling seemed less enthusiastic.

> A noble dish is that scrapple, but don't eat three slices and go to work straight on top of 'em. That's the way to dyspepsia! 🦋

Edward Bok, *The Americanization of Edward Bok: An Autobiography*, (Philadelphia: Consolidates/Drake Press, 1920) p. 153.

The Constitutional
Centennial
1887

In 1837, when the American government decided
to celebrate the writing and adoption of its most
significant document, the Golden Jubilee of the
Constitution attracted little interest. According to Michael
Kammen, author of *A Machine That Would Go of Itself: The
Constitution in American Culture*, the most memorable event
of the alleged celebration was a New York Historical Soci-
ety-sponsored affair at which poet William Cullen Bryant
presented an ode commissioned for the event that was so
mediocre that he didn't allow it to be published in later
editions of his work. Even worse was a two-hour speech
from John Quincy Adams.

Interest in the Constitution declined even further from
there. But without a national holiday like the 4th of July
(which bolstered interest in the Declaration of Indepen-

Michael Kammen, *A Machine That Would Go of Itself: The Constitution in American Culture* (New York: Random House, 1986), pp.
127–151.

dence), September 17 meant nothing to the average American. In 1882, J. Franklin Jameson, a constitutional scholar,
found the document folded up in a tin box in a closet of the
library of the State Department in Washington while the
Declaration of Independence was proudly displayed. This
was not a good sign.

Still, Philadelphia decided to have a celebration for
the Constitution's one hundredth birthday. The response
was underwhelming; the few states that did care argued over
the date to celebrate and the right of Philadelphia to host the
event. Every state and territory was invited to send a representative to Philadelphia on December 2, 1886, to help orga-
nize the events. Only twenty-seven out of forty-seven
showed up.

Those that did come made some important decisions
about the festivities. They decided that the President should
participate; that a major oration should be read and a com-
memorative poem presented; that military and industrial
presentations should be made; and that a permanent monument should be created.

Within weeks, members of the committee began to
grumble that nothing was happening with the plans. Fingers
pointed to Congressman John A. Kasson of Iowa, who had
been elected president of the commission and was notorious
for missing meetings. At one point he wrote that he would
come to town if "there is a cool place to stay near Phil. I
must have cool nights for sleep."

Letters were sent on June 15, 1887, inviting representatives from the states and telling them that they would have

to transport their own troops. A response was requested by July 1. In a case of too little too late, the committee responded to grumblings by the states by offering fifty cents per man for each of their three days in Philadelphia. The offer didn't help.

Among those who showed a marked disinterest in the celebration was President Grover Cleveland. After receiving his invitation, he refused to commit to one state's celebration, noting the different dates that ratification took place. "I do not feel warranted in discriminating in favor of or against the propositions to select one day or place in preference to all others . . . " noted the Commander-in-Chief. But Cleveland had a change of heart and ultimately did show up for the requisite banquets, speeches, and glad-handing.

The second part of the original plan proved less successful. Chief Justice Morrison Waite, New York Senator Roscoe Conkling, Cornell University President Andrew Dickson, and others initially accepted then declined the invitation to be the event's official orator. Associate Justice Samuel Miller, nobody's first choice, accepted.

As for the poetry post, Camden resident Walt Whitman was thought too controversial. Everyone else who was invited passed on the offer. When New England poet John Greenleaf Whittier added his name to the pass list, the committee decided there would be no official poet.

Parades were held, which satisfied the third part of the plan. But more trouble arose with point four: the creation of a permanent monument. In 1890, three years after the celebration, a design still had not been decided upon. By then, the monument's mission was redefined. If it ever did get designed and built, it would represent not only the Constitution but also the Declaration of Independence, the new government of 1789, and other historical events. Even these watered-down plans were ultimately abandoned, leaving the city with no monument to its most significant document. 🦋

A War on Drugs

1892

For years ads for miracle elixirs and cure-all tonics had been making the nation's leading magazines look like today's *Weekly World News*. Government regulation had yet to be enacted, and the Post Office had no restrictions on the ingredients of these mail-order drugs. Publishers around the country eager for the income accepted such ads without question.

But in 1892, one Philadelphia publisher, Cyrus H. K. Curtis, decided to face the scourge head on. His weapon: *The Ladies Home Journal.*

Under the editorial eye of Edward Bok, the *Journal* set out to be more than just a proving ground for recipes and sewing tips. Curtis and Bok decided to make an issue out of fighting the patent medicines no matter what damage it did to their wallets.

First, Curtis banned ads for such products. But his battle went beyond advertising.

One early target was Lydia E. Pinkham Vegetable Compound, advertised as a panacea for female woes. In advertisements, the manufacturers claimed that "Miss Lydia" herself was cloistered in her laboratory improving the compound. Curtis printed a photo of Miss Lydia's gravestone, where she had been buried twenty-two years earlier.

The *Journal* also did in Mrs. Winslow's Soothing Syrup by purchasing a bottle in London, where labeling was mandatory under the English Pharmacy Act. Although the manufacturers denied the presence of morphine, the British label stated otherwise.

A minor setback in this drug war occurred when Bok published a list of twenty-seven medicines and their ingredients. One irate manufacturer, whose product Bok said contained opium, although, in fact, it didn't, sued the magazine and was awarded $16,000.

The *Journal* recovered quickly, enlisting the aid of New York lawyer Mark Sullivan, who gave up his practice to work on exposing the nineteenth-century drug lords. Sullivan revealed the shocking fact that for their own perverse pleasure, many companies were circulating the personal letters women had confidentially sent in to the company graphically describing their "private ailments."

Within two years, seven other newspapers and magazines, as well as the Women's Christian Temperance Union, joined Curtis in the fight. By 1906, public support and pressure-group influence was so strong that Congress passed the Federal Food and Drug Act. By that time, however, the *Journal* had moved on to a new scandalous subject—venereal disease. ✹

Goldman's Bust

1893

Anarchist Emma Goldman was arrested in 1893 in Philadelphia as she was about to speak to a gathering of the unemployed. The previous day, Goldman had delivered one of her most famous speeches, telling a crowd in New York.

> Ask for work. If they do not give you work, ask for bread. If they do not give you work or bread, then take bread.

New York police alerted Philadelphia that this dangerous woman was on her way.

An observer recalled:

> You should have seen how they feared [her] in Philadelphia. They got out a whole platoon of police and detectives and executed a military maneuver to catch [her]. And when she walked up to them, then they surrounded and captured her, and guarded the City Hall where they kept her overnight, and put a detective next to her cell to make notes. ✄

The First Docudrama

1897

Siegmund Lubin started in the motion picture business in 1890, at a time when most people weren't even aware that there was a motion-picture business.

But Lubin managed to turn his optical shop on Eighth Street near Market Street into one of the world's largest motion picture companies long before Universal and Columbia Pictures entered the industry. Although his success was evident, his methods were sometimes questionable.

On March 17, 1897, "Gentleman" Jim Corbett, heavyweight boxing champion of the world, faced a challenge from British-born Bob Fitzsimmons in a Carson City, Nevada, stadium built especially for the bout. As the crowd cheered, the two circled, bobbed, and jabbed. There was blood flying by the eighth round, but the battle didn't end until the fourteenth round, when Fitzsimmons delivered a blow to the solar plexus that stunned Corbett. After the count, Corbett lunged at his usurper and had to be restrained by officials. It was dramatic stuff, as anticipated by the camera crews on hand to record the event.

The fight, in fact, had been financed by a group of

filmmakers, the Veriscope Company, which also owned the rights to release a movie of the event. Veriscope announced that the film would be ready for release by May, two months after the bout.

Lubin knew about the Veriscope film. He also knew that the film version would surely entertain the novice moviegoers who were accustomed to tamer fare, such as his company's titles, which then included *Lady Contortionist* and *Unveiling of the Great Monument at Philadelphia*. And so, denied the rights to shoot the real thing, Lubin decided on the next best thing: to stage and record a recreation of the fight.

His actors were freight handlers from the Pennsylvania terminal. The location was the roof of Lubin's studios at 910 Arch Street. For a script, he used a newspaper account of the fight that was read to the actors round by round by an off-screen prompter.

Soon after the two laborers slugged it out for fourteen rounds, Lubin began advertising that his film, titled *The Great Corbett-Fitzsimmons Fight (in counterpart)*, would be ready by April, a month before the film of the actual fight would be distributed.

The Veriscope Company was not happy and threatened Lubin, stating that "anyone buying these bogus films will not be permitted to exhibit them." But the law favored Lubin, who managed to get a copyright on his facsimile. Without realizing it, he had created one of the first docudramas—a re-creation of an event using actors and a set.

In the coming years Lubin would take this questionable practice a step further. Instead of going to the trouble of re-enacting the work of others, he would simply make bootleg copies of their work and sell them as his own. Lubin, who died in 1923, was not only one of the film industries first "pirates," but also one of its early millionaires.

Jeanes's Will

1907

The First African Baptist Church was in the right place at the right time. Situated on Cherry Street just below 11th, it happened to be directly behind the property of Miss Anna T. Jeanes.

During the late 1890s, the Arch Street resident took an interest in the church and its congregation and helped lead it to prosperity. By the time Jeanes left her family home, the church had enough cash flow to abandon its old site and built a new church at 16th and Christian.

Jeanes's father, Isaac Jeanes, was a merchant. One of her brothers was a cofounder of Hahnemann Medical College. On the death of her brothers and father, Jeanes inherited millions.

In April of 1906, she gave $1 million of her family

"Memories Haunt Jeanes Homestead," *Philadelphia Evening Bulletin*, February 14, 1921. "Answers to Queries," *Philadelphia Evening Bulletin*, September 20, 1952. "Miss Jeanes's Death Due to Old Age, *Philadelphia Evening Bulletin*, September 25, 1907. "Charities May Get Jeanes Million," *Philadelphia Press*, September 26, 1907. "Anna T. Jeanes Dead," *New York Times*, September 25, 1907. "Miss Jeanes Gives 5 Million Away," *Philadelphia Evening Bulletin*, September 30, 1907. "Miss Jeanes's Funeral," *Bulletin*, September 27, 1907.

fortune to help black children in the rural South (among the trustees of the fund was Booker T. Washington, then of Tuskegee Institute).

When she died the following year, her will featured a remarkable list of charitable contributions. There was another $5 million for the education of black children as well as $200,000 for Friends Schools, and $100,000 to Hahnemann Hospital. She even started a Jeanes Fund to distribute money to those who wished to be cremated for free. Originally this was limited to those to be interred in the Fair Hill Burial Grounds in Germantown but the offer was later reinterpreted to include cremation at other sites.

The strangest part of her bequest, though, involved Swarthmore College. The will stated:

> I conditionally give, devise and bequeath to Swarthmore College my coal lands and mineral rights in the State of Pennsylvania together with my five-eighth ownership in the Rebecca Steadman tract (Hazlebrook Colliery).

Then came the catch.

> on condition that the management of the aforesaid Swarthmore College shall discontinue and abandon all participation in intercollegiate sports and games, but should the management of Swarthmore College fail to accept and carry out these conditions, I will and direct that the aforesaid coal lands, mineral rights and ownership shall be sold and the proceeds shall be included and merged in the assets of the estate.

In other words, she meant business.

Joseph Swain, president of Swarthmore, was a bit surprised when he heard about the generous gift. According to a contemporary newspaper account, "He said that he preferred to make no comment as to the probable action the college would take until he had time to digest the rather astonishing news."

Shortly thereafter, the college announced that it had rejected the bequest. ✖

Custody Battles

1909

An illegal marriage, two custody fights, an asylum escape, a kidnapping, a $3 million will. . . . No, it isn't a new made-for-TV movie, it's the saga of Zaida McDonald, and one of the city's most spectacular domestic battles.

Zaida was already separated for four years from her husband, Camden shipping magnate Francis J. McDonald, when, in 1909, one of their sons died of spinal meningitis. The despondent Mrs. McDonald was barred from the funeral by her husband, who claimed she would get hysterical and make a scene. Determined to see her child one last time, she discovered the location of the services. But on the way there her car broke down, giving her no choice but to run a mile before getting another ride. When she got to the church, the doors were locked and she was forced to climb through a window.

A few days later, Francis consulted with two doctors and had his wife committed to the Burn Brae Asylum in Clifton Heights—this despite her physician's claim that she was perfectly sane.

But Zaida did not stay institutionalized for long. While

she was on one of her regular evening walks, a sedan pulled up on the asylum grounds. Private detectives leaped out, restrained Zaida's nurse, and spirited away the grateful inmate. Although he threatened to press charges, Francis let the matter drop. But the subject of her stay at the asylum arose again when, during their divorce proceedings, Zaida used her husband's actions as leverage to get custody of their remaining son, Francis, Jr. Once again, Zaida's determination won out, and she got custody of the boy.

Twenty-one years later, the McDonald story took another strange turn. By then, Francis Jr., had married and given Zaida a granddaughter, Eleanor Francis "Dolly" McDonald. But soon Dolly's mother, Eleanor, divorced Francis Jr., and was awarded custody of Dolly.

Quickly the mother remarried, became Eleanor Stuart, and put the six-year-old in a boarding school. Zaida believed that her granddaughter was not in the best of hands. And so while little Dolly's mother and stepfather were on their honeymoon, Grandmom Zaida drove up to the school, took Dolly, and sped away. The child remained, uncontested, in her grandmother's care—until Francis Sr., Zaida's ex-husband, died.

In his will, he left $3 million to the child. That's when Eleanor Stuart decided to reclaim custody of her daughter. Yet another custody battle erupted, this time between mother and grandmother. During one particularly tearful afternoon of testimony, it was revealed that Mrs. Stuart had married Mr. Stuart even before she was legally divorced from her first husband. Zaida also accused the child's mother of hosting drunken house parties, and contended that the custody battle started only after the inheritance was announced. But none of that was enough to sway the court. Even Francis Jr., for whose custody Zaida had fought so tenaciously years earlier, claimed that, in his opinion, the child would be better off with his ex-wife than with his mother. The court agreed.

Embittered, Zaida McDonald left the courtroom announcing, "This is terrible. . . . I'd rather bury her than see her go to that woman." ✹

An Ordinance for Pinheads

1910

In 1910, an ordinance that attempted to regulate the size of ladies' hatpins died in committee, thanks in part to opinions like that of Councilman Alfred Gratz.

Rather than fear the fashion accessory as a weapon, Gratz called the hatpin "woman's best friend" as well as their best defense against mashers.

Thin Air

1911

In January of 1911, former postmaster of Philadelphia Richard L. Ashhurst, a Naples-born Civil War veteran, decided on the spur of the moment to visit Atlantic City.

The seventy-two-year old man checked into the Marlborough-Blenheim Hotel with his son, John. He telegraphed his wife, saying:

Came to Atlantic City unexpectedly. Quite well.
Will explain by letter. Home early tomorrow.

Around 8:45 he took a ride on a boardwalk rolling chair, joked with the driver, got off at Million Dollar Pier, and was never seen again. 🦋

A Night to Remember

1912

When the *S.S. Titanic* struck an iceberg off the coast of Newfoundland on April 14, 1912, Bryn Mawr man-about-town William Carter lost twenty-four polo sticks, sixty shirts, fifteen pairs of shoes, two sets of tails, and his Renault motorcar. He also, figuratively, lost his family. But unlike the icy collision, this loss may not have been accidental.

In the chaos that ensued when the *Titanic* went down, Carter was separated from his wife, Lucille Polk Carter, and their two children. They were reunited the next day, aboard the vessel *Carpathia*, which was providing a safe haven for the survivors. After the rescue, the Carters chose to keep a low profile, and none of the clan except ten-year-old Billy spoke to the press:

> All the boys and girls were with the women and while the people were getting into the boats a man would try to break through the line and then there would be some shooting.

Little Billy's observations were particularly interesting in light of his father's actions.

In New York on his way home, William Carter made a scene by knocking down a reporter who asked him how he managed to escape in a boatful of women. After all, 1,500 people were not so lucky. The Senate investigating committee was interested in the same questions. William Carter, it turned out, absent his wife and children, had somehow gotten onto the same lifeboat as Bruce Ismay, president of the White Star Line, owner of the *Titanic*. It was rumored that theirs was the first lifeboat to leave the ship. Charges of cowardice arose but were later dropped.

The matter rested until January of 1914, when Mrs. Carter sued her husband for divorce on the grounds of "cruel and barbarous treatment and indignities to the person." Friends speculated that the Carters' problems stemmed from the *Titanic* incident, but they would not elaborate. Although every effort was made to keep the proceedings and testimony quiet, at least some of Mrs. Carter's accusations reached the press.

According to her testimony:

When the *Titanic* struck, my husband came to our stateroom and said, "Get up and dress yourself and the children." I never saw him again until I arrived at the *Carpathia* at 8 o'clock the next morning, when I saw him leaning on the rail. All he said was that he had had a jolly good breakfast and that he never thought I would make it.

Although William Carter denied abandoning his clan that night, saying that he made every effort to take care of his family, the judge concluded that the case was "an almost unparalleled citation of a husband's depravity."

Insult was added to humiliation when, over a year after the divorce was granted, Carter was sued by a Paris fashion buyer for garments purchased but not paid for by the former Mrs. Carter just before the final decree. ✹

True Confessions

1924

s long as I am president of Princeton University, there is no place for Buchmanism at Princeton.

So announced Dr. John Grier Hibben in 1924. Hibben assumed that he had heard the last of Buchmanism's influence over the Philadelphian Society, Princeton's campus Christian group. But two years later the cult was thriving again, and Hibben found himself squaring off once more against the popular movement.

But what was Buchmanism?

According to Frank N. D. Buchman, born in Pennsburg, Pennsylvania, a graduate of the Mt. Airy Seminary, and former pastor of Overbrook's Church of the Good Shepherd:

> If you have real love for men you should be willing to share your temptations with them. You should be willing to confess your secret thoughts, to get alongside of their souls to work with them to the end of redemption.

What all that translated to was a cult built around a charismatic preacher, one who heavily emphasized public confessions of immorality and sexual transgressions. These

119

confessions were made during weekend gatherings led by "soul surgeons" who goaded the sinners into detailed recounting of their sordid deeds.

It was not simply the notion of confession that bothered Hibben and his Princeton compatriots. They were distressed by what Hibben termed "an approach to religion through an exaggerated emotional appeal with undue emphasis on sex."

While the Princeton crackdown occurred, Buchman was getting more attention by hobnobbing with Queen Marie of Rumania, who was reported to be impressed with Buchman's doctrines.

As the Princeton incident became a footnote to Buchman's career, his involvement with world leaders became better known. In later years, Buchmanism evolved into "Moral Re-Armament," which received worldwide attention.

"Moral Re-Armament is doing for Africa what George Washington did for America," said Ghana's largest daily newspaper. "Most people load me down with problems," said Filipino president Ramon Magsaysay to Buchman. "You bring me the answers." In 1951, Buchman was nominated for the Nobel Peace Prize on the strength of his crusade.

Buchman's oddest convert probably was Mae West, who, in 1939, announced, "I owe my success to the fact that I have been practicing this philosophy in recent years." She also suggested that he attempt to help her friend, Philadelphia-native, W. C. Fields.

"I'd love to," replied Buchman, but Field never became re-armed.   ✷✷

A New Chief in Town,

PART 2

1925

The knowledge that this great general is to be director of public safety will be notice to all evildoers and law violators that Philadelphia will be a most unhealthy place for their operation.

So said Mayor W. Freeland Kendrick in December 1923.

The subject of his praise was General Smedley Darlington Butler, one of the few out-of-towners ever to lead Philadelphia's police force. He had come to the city at the special request of Governor Gifford Pinchot and newly elected Mayor Kendrick, who had approached President Calvin Coolidge for the loan of the general to help curb Philadelphia's crime problem.

Butler took the position and the mayor's threats to the criminal element very seriously. Within his first week in office, an unprecedented six hundred speakeasies were shut down and two thousand people were arrested. The general's zeal made it an uncomfortable time for many politicians, and the feathers he ruffled brought about standoffs with the city treasurer, ward leaders, city magistrates, and the courts. Of the six thousand arrested for Prohibition violations in Butler's second year in office, only two hundred and twelve were convicted.

"The path of law enforcement has been blocked by powerful influences, by legal machinery that should have been an aid, and by the invocation of technicalities," he lamented. Still, he requested another year to clean up Philadelphia.

President Coolidge told Butler that his request was denied. But Butler was still intent on completing the prosecution of three major Center City hotels all charged with violations of the liquor laws. (Kendrick himself was believed to be responsible for the delay once the cases got to court). So Butler defied Coolidge and announced that he was resigning from the Marine Corps so he could continue in Philadelphia.

This came as a shock to Kendrick, who promptly fired Butler. Chagrined at his sudden unemployment, Butler made some defiant noises to reporters, but in the end he packed his belongings and left City Hall.

On December 29, 1925, the Marine Corps announced that it would allow Butler to return to his position as brigadier general. After a month's vacation, he was assigned to a base in California.

The two-time Congressional Medal of Honor winner once said: "Trying to enforce the law in Philadelphia is worse than any battle I was ever in." ✶

At War with the
Walk-ins
1926

When Philadelphia's most famous acting son, John Barrymore, noted excessive coughing in an audience while he was performing, he returned for act two with a large fish which he tossed into the audience. "Here, you damned walruses," he was quoted as saying, "busy yourselves with this, while we go on with the play."

When Philadelphia Orchestra maestro Leopold Stokowski faced similar problems, he handled things with greater grace and more creativity than the tempestuous Barrymore.

The musical program selected for the afternoon concert of April 16, 1926, was a bit unusual—an obscure *Fantasie* by Guillaume Lekeu; Wagner's "Ride of the Valkyries" and "Woton's Farewell"; a selection of songs by Brahms and; to climax, Haydn's *Farewell Symphony*. But to the unsuspecting matinee audience, it seemed to be just another example

Peter Hay, *Theatrical Anecdotes* (New York: Oxford University Press, 1987), p. 259.

of their beloved conductor's eclectic selections. For Stokow-ski, who, in his reign over the Philadelphia Orchestra, had waged constant battles against over-anxious applauders and compulsive coughers, it was payback time.

The concert began with only the sounds of a cello and the first violin, as called for by the composer. The rest of the seats on stage were empty. As the piece required, the other instruments were added gradually, but under Stokowski's scheme, the musicians waited in the wings until just before they were needed. Then they walked on stage, took their seats, and began playing. This continued until the small orchestra needed for the piece was completely assembled.

When the music stopped, the ushers opened the doors and those who had arrived late poured down the aisles, uncertain why they were getting so much attention.

They soon realized when "Ride of the Valkyries" be-gan and the rest of the orchestra suddenly rushed to their seats on stage. Breathless brasses hurried into position as the conductor lowered his baton. More musicians filed onto the stage, checking their watches and hurrying to arrange their sheet music.

The program continued normally, except for an un-expected early exit by the flutes who weren't needed after the first of the Brahms songs.

Stokowski took his final dig at the crowd that day by taking Haydn's *Farewell Symphony* literally. As a reporter observed:

> The first movement had just got underway when
> one or two members of the orchestra apparently

tired of playing, calmly quit, folded their music and wandered off the stage. This kept up, until, in the last movement, only two violins remained.

They, too, left after finishing.

At the end of the concert, Stokowski looked out over the empty stage and signaled the vanished orchestra to take a bow. Then he turned and, without acknowledging that any point had been made at all, took his own bow and walked off. ✹

Climbing the Walls

1926

In 1926, "human fly" and steeplejack Harry H. Gardiner, age fifty-six, climbed the north side of Philadelphia City Hall as part of a fund-raising drive. He arrived at the top of William Penn's hat two hours and ten minutes after he left the ground. 🦟

The Bizarre Case of
Dr. Eldridge

1927

There's not much information about Thomas Edwin Eldridge at the University of Pennsylvania's Medical Library. There is only passing mention of him in the reference collection at the College of Physicians.

But in the early 1900s when Eldridge practiced medicine out of his North Broad Street office, this unusual doctor had no trouble getting his name in print. In 1907, he faced accusations of hiring a detective to murder his wife. In 1910, he got lost for four days while floating over New Jersey and New York (Eldridge was one of Philadelphia's foremost balloonists). Nine years later he installed a huge clock above his Logan Square residence to tell young girls in the park across the street that it might be time to go home to bed.

But his entry in the 1927 *Who's Who in Philadelphia* doesn't mention any of these exploits under the doctor's distinguished portrait. What it does mention, rather casually, is Eldridge's involvement with a strange series of experiments in his supposed specialty, something called "electro-therapeutics."

Eldridge was, according to *Who's Who*, "the first man to note that the X-ray would turn the flesh of a Negro to a lighter color." These bizarre experiments with skin pigmentation were conducted in 1903 when Eldridge theorized that the same treatment used on port wine stains and birthmarks could also be used to treat blacks who were "anxious to become lighter." After a volunteer was found, Eldridge applied daily doses of X-rays and radium, beginning on the man's back.

Eldridge reported:

> The Negro upon whom we are experimenting is anxious to become lighter, and if he will continue under the treatment, I am confident that he will become white. I also intend to secure some monkeys shortly upon which I will make similar experiments.

After taking credit for turning the man's back and abdomen a color that would "make an albino jealous," he admitted to reporters, "Some doubts still exist in my mind as to the effect of the treatment upon the skin." His doubts notwithstanding, he added, "I hope, however, within a month the man will be completely white."

What happened to Eldridge's human guinea pig is unknown. But the doctor himself made headlines again three years later—for practicing medicine without a license. It was then that the president of the state medical board, Dr. Henry Beates, launched an attack on Eldridge and other "fakirs who traffic in human life." The trail brought to light not only Eldridge's skin experiments, but also one other equally startling claim—that he had the ability to raise the dead. ✄

The Hit

1927

ou're that tough guy from Philadelphia," a gutsy Chicago mobster was reported to have commented when he observed gangland kingpin William "Mickey" Duffy giving a fiver to a hat-check girl at a New York nightclub. "Why don't you give the girl some real money?"

"I'll give her real money," replied Duffy. He gave her a ten, then said to his new acquaintance, "If you need charity, here's a ten for you."

The brawl that followed resulted in a cut scalp for Duffy and a week in the hospital for his rival. Not long after the incident, word was out that Duffy had been marked for revenge.

And so when, in February 1927, Duffy heard that the Chicago boys were coming to Philadelphia, he made plans to spend a few days in Hot Springs, Arkansas.

But before leaving, he couldn't resist a visit to the Club Cadix, at 2320 Chestnut Street, a popular nightspot with a reputation for bootleg whiskey and risque dancers. While he and his entourage were inside dancing, witnesses outside saw an automobile park near a line of taxis. In the early hours of the morning, Duffy, his wife, and his bodyguard, John Bricker, left the club and walked across the sidewalk to their car. As Bricker opened the car door for Mrs. Duffy, the mysterious car suddenly raced down Chestnut Street. Before Duffy or Bricker could get off a single shot, both were riddled with bullets. Blood flowed for fifty feet along the snow-covered curb.

A pair of taxi drivers rushed out of a nearby restaurant, put the two men in their cabs, and drove them to Hahnemann Hospital. Bricker was pronounced dead-on-arrival with eight bullet wounds. Duffy, who had been hit seven times in the forehead, neck, abdomen, thigh, and cheek, wasn't expected to survive, either. A Catholic priest administered the last rites, and the cops asked Duffy who had done the shooting. "I'm too weak to talk much," he replied, "but you know if I could talk, I wouldn't tell you a thing."

Duffy's lack of cooperation didn't discourage the police. This was the first time machine guns had been used for murder in the city, and the department was adamant about keeping it from happening again.

In the course of the next six weeks; Duffy miraculously recovered and was released from the hospital; the Club Cadix was sold after being closed for alcohol violations; and hoods Petey Ford and Frankie Bailey, among others, were arrested in connection with the machine-gun attack.

Duffy survived until 1931, when another gang of assassins killed him while he slept in his suite at the Ambassador Hotel in Atlantic City. ✣

The Palace of Depression

1932

To anyone else in the 1930s driving down Vineland's Mill Road, it looked like nothing but an old auto graveyard and swamp. But to ex-gold miner George Daynor, it was all he needed to create a South Jersey architectural wonder—the Palace of Depression.

With all the subtlety of an Old Testament prophet (and a hairstyle to match), Daynor proclaimed that, led by angels, he had outwitted the devil to find this special spot. For three years, under cover of night, Daynor hammered and cemented together broken auto fenders, pots and pans, wood, branches, and other assorted junk he found on his property. In 1932, in the midst of the Great Depression, he opened his masterpiece to an unsuspecting public.

"This is proof of externalized thought," explained Daynor as he led tourists at ten cents a head through his new home. He showed them the peepholes he had made in his sewer pipe (to watch for the devil), allowed them to swing an Irish shillelagh, and pointed out the tree-stump stools and the California sunset–style arched ceilings (covered with homemade paint).

He would not show visitors the spooky subterranean cavern where he claimed to live. But he did allow them to gaze at "the greatest idea and most unique door ever conceived by man," which was made out of a wagon wheel, cement, and broken bottles.

The Palace of Depression remained one of Vineland's big attractions until July 4, 1956, when an infant was kidnapped from his Long Island home. The eighty-one-year-old Daynor thought he could get some publicity for his palace out of this unfortunate incident and called popular syndicated columnist Walter Winchell. Daynor told him that the kidnappers had visited the Palace of Depression and offered to return the baby for $5,000.

The FBI was not amused. Daynor found himself sentenced to a year in prison for supplying false and misleading information. When he was released, he moved back into the palace but never again opened it to the public. In 1961, he was found suffering from malnutrition and taken to a hospital. He died on October 20, 1964.

The house was damaged by fire that year. After Daynor's death, it was used primarily for high school drinking parties. It has since been demolished.

"The only real depression," said this unsung visionary, "is a depression of individual ingenuity. . . . If you don't have originality, you get lost in the shuffle. 🦋

Getting a Monopoly on Monopoly

1933

Charles B. Darrow of Germantown invented the game Monopoly during the Depression primarily to amuse himself. When it came to naming the streets, he naturally adopted those of his favorite vacation spot—Atlantic City.

Darrow gave the game to friends and sold it in Philadelphia. Demand grew and Darrow ultimately approached Parker Brothers, to whom he sold the rights to the game.

Or so says the introduction to the game rules that are included with all the rest (the deeds and tiny metal cannons, race cars, and Scotties) in every Monopoly box.

But Darrow had less to do with the invention of Monopoly than Parker Brothers would have players believe. According to Philip Orbanes in his obsessive book, *The Monopoly Companion*, Elizabeth Magie patented something called "The Landlord's Game" in 1904. A strong proponent

Philip Orbanes, *The Monopoly Companion* (New York: Adams, Inc., 1988).

of the elimination of all taxes but real estate (a theory expounded by economist Henry George), Magie developed the board game as a form of propaganda against big business. It was sold in homemade editions throughout eastern Pennsylvania, where it eventually became popular on college campuses, including the University of Pennsylvania and Haverford College. The Landlord's Game included such familiar Monopoly features as a luxury-tax space, a jail, a go-to-jail space, and numerous properties for sale.

In 1924 Magie approached Parker Brothers, the publisher of her previous game Mock Trail. But toy czar George Parker turned down The Landlord's Game. It just wasn't any fun.

A remarkably similar game, Finance, which emerged in the Midwest during the early 1930s, included many of the same spaces as The Landlord's Game but added cards labeled "Community Chest" and "Chance." It seems that the "inventor" of Finance, Dan Layman, had played The Landlord's Game while in college.

Here's where Darrow, who actually lived in Mt. Airy, got involved. Layman played his game with a man who later played it with one Ruth Hoskins. Hoskins altered the board to include Atlantic City properties when she moved to New Jersey. She then played her game with some folks, among them one Charles Todd.

Todd then brought the game to the house of a former high school classmate, Esther Darrow. She and her husband Charles first played the game in 1933.

Darrow did some fiddling of his own with the game.

He kept all of the Atlantic City street names (including the misspelled Marvin Gardens) but added illustrations. He reorganized some of the rules and then had the game copyrighted. A year later, he approached Parker Brothers. At first they rejected the game, but when Darrow sold large numbers of the game on his own, they bought the idea (as well as the patents to both The Landlord's Game and Finance).

And since 1953, when both of those patents ran out, Charles Darrow has gotten sole credit for inventing Monopoly. ✄

Baker's Billions

1934

J acob Baker, an early American settler, owned vast tracts of land in Philadelphia, including the grounds under Independence Hall and the Pennsylvania Railway Terminal. His holdings also included an entire small town in Ohio.

Approximately eleven thousand acres were granted to Baker in recognition of his service in the Revolutionary War and the War of 1812. When Baker died in 1840, his will stipulated that the land, which carried a 1930s value of between $1.8 and $3 billion, was to be turned over to his son, Peter, and his daughter, Elizabeth. After their deaths, the lands became the legitimate property of their descendants. The lease on the land expired near the end of 1920, which would make thousands of Baker descendants rich.

At least that's what more than three thousand Bakers

"Lay Claim to Ohio City," *New York Times*, February 15, 1921. "Baker Will Claimants 'Duped,'" *New York Times*, October 6, 1934. "U.S. Indicts Thirty in Baker Will Fraud," *Philadelphia Evening Bulletin*, December 15, 1934. "Indict 30 for Part in 'Estate' Fraud," *New York Times*, December 16, 1936. "Baker Estate Up Again," *New York Times*, March 13, 1938.

were told when they received notification in the mail of their long lost forefather. To get closer to the inheritance rightly due them, the Bakers were asked to send back a list of their living relatives and a sum to help finance the work of settling the estate. Charts in the mailing showed how each Baker was a descendant of Jacob.

Spirits were high and checks were written until October 6, 1934, when the claimants were told by Philadelphia solicitor for the Register of Wills Robert M. Boyle that they had been duped. "It is extremely doubtful whether there is any actual estate at all," he said. Thirty people were eventually indicted by a federal grand jury for the mail fraud. 🦋

The Spite Fence

1935

Shibe Park (later Connie Mack Stadium) opened in 1909, and if you lived across from the stadium and you dragged a lawn chair and a six-pack up to your roof, you could enjoy a clear view of the Philadelphia Athletics over the low right-field fence.

Some neighbors were downright enterprising. These folks discovered that a good-sized roof on North 20th Street could bring in quite a few fans at twenty-five to fifty cents a head. Even more could be seated if you built bleachers, which many did. Business boomed on the roofs while residents fought off attacks by the fire marshal, who claimed the homemade bleachers were unsafe, and the city solicitor, who wanted the roofs declared "places of public amusement" and regulated and taxed accordingly. Having a house on 20th Street was particularly profitable during a World Series. For the 1929 Series, homeowners charged $1 to $5 a head. Kids got a piece of the action, too, by buying five-cent hot dogs from street vendors and reselling them on the roof for double the price.

During a winning A's season, higher ticket prices could

be charged both inside and outside the ballpark, making it worthwhile to put up with cracks in the ceiling and additional roof repairs. Real estate and rental values went up on these properties thanks to the unique upstairs situation. One homeowner, Charles Harvey, didn't even bother renting his house. He decided it was more profitable just to use it for game-day seating.

The A's management initially attempted to be diplomatic with their entrepreneurial neighbors. They had no problem with the rooftop bleacher business so long as all the bleachers inside Shibe Park were filled. Problems came when the roof seats filled up but the stadium didn't (a situation similar to today's television black outs of those home games that don't sell a predetermined number of seats in the stadium).

The team proposed an agreement that would permit rooftop seating only during sold-out games. The entrepreneurs on 20th Street balked at that compromise. More drastic action was called for. And so, where city ordinances and threats by team officials failed, fifty feet of corrugated iron succeeded. After the 1934 season, the A's decided to raise the right-field wall from twelve to fifty feet high. Called a "spite fence" by residents, the wall made it impossible for those across the street to see the field.

Four thousand fans braved bitter cold to watch the 1935 season opener from inside the stadium. The neighbors got only a hint of what was happening inside when three home runs come lofting over the newly enlarged right-field wall to their doorsteps.

Many were suddenly outraged by their proximity to major-league baseball. Complained Catherine O'Donnell:

> The windows in my house have been broken any
> number of times by home runs and practice hits.
> This whole street becomes a wreck in summer when
> the rooters go through it in droves. And still I don't
> mind. But this fence is too much.

Most, however, accepted the wall quietly. "What's the difference?" asked one defeated entrepreneur who had dismantled his bleachers. Since the A's had gone downhill, it was getting hard to sell rooftop seats anyway. No one wanted to see the game. "By that time the rooftop trade was shot," one historian noted, "and so was Connie Mack's team."

A Fascist Parade Flap
1936

In 1936, Philadelphia's chapter of the Sons of Italy thought it had a fitting reason to celebrate. Benito Mussolini's forces had at last captured Addis Ababa, the capital city of Ethiopia. To show their support, the group decided that on May 10th they would march through Philadelphia.

And so they asked the city for a parade permit.

The day before the scheduled event, Mayor S. Davis Wilson met with the parade organizers. Fearing possible rioting and bloodshed, he announced that the march was off. He would be damned if he would permit such a parade to occur, he said, throwing his glasses down on his desk. So intense were the mayor's objections, in fact, that his glasses rebounded off his desk and struck one of his visitors in the face.

Meanwhile, a group of anti-Fascist Italian-Americans entered City Hall to support Wilson's move against the parade. The group was ushered into the office of the director of public safety, a safe distance away from where the mayor addressed the pro-paraders.

The parade's main backers were John M. di Silvestro, a personal friend of Premier Mussolini, and Francesco Pelosi, an Italian-American who fought with the United States in World War I. They demanded their right to parade, pointing out that even the Communists had been allowed to march and hold meetings at Reyburn Plaza.

But Mayor Wilson was adamant. "If I granted such a permit I would not be able to sleep," he said. Finally, a compromise was reached: The Mussolini supporters would be allowed to hold a mass meeting instead of a parade.

Di Silvestro wasn't overly pleased with the compromise. He objected to his group being treated like children, but finally left the office peacefully. "Very well. We will show that we are as good American citizens as all others," he sniffed. And then he withdrew his permit request and, believing his point had been made, called off the mass meeting, too. ✄

Franklin's Fan

1937

It was a great human interest story: a hometown kid so adoring of President Franklin Delano Roosevelt that he wore out his old shoes walking to Franklin Field to witness the president's speech to the Democratic National Convention.

Once the boy managed to get in, he ate, bought souvenirs, heard FDR, and fell asleep. When he woke up, it was 4:30 A.M. and his parents had reported him missing. Some cleaning men finally helped him home, and the kid's story made the papers. Roosevelt got wind of it, and the kid soon received a surprise package in the mail—a new pair of black oxfords to replace his old ones, and a letter from the chief executive's secretary.

But nine months later, in May 1937, the kid wasn't so cute. His adventures weren't so adorable and his spunk was less than admirable. Eight-year-old Jimmy Brady's troubles began shortly after his encounter with the president. First, he was picked up for breaking into an apartment and two fraternity houses to steal empty beer bottles and cigarette lighters. "Gee, I sure hope the president forgives me," he was quoted as saying, "'cause he's a pretty good friend of mine."

A few months later, Jimmy struck a woman and was ordered by the court to be committed to reform school.

Before he was committed, however, Jimmy went walking through the Woodlands Cemetery and met seven-year-old John S. Tighe, Jr. John was visiting his grandmother on Mother's Day and was wearing a carnation in his lapel. Jimmy wasn't impressed.

Soon after encountering John, Jimmy returned home and told his parents that John and he were chased by two boys with rifles, one of whom pushed John into the Schuylkill. Jimmy didn't have much of a reputation for honesty, and it wasn't long before skeptical adults got him to admit the truth.

Jimmy finally confessed:

> [The two boys] got to fooling around and I slapped him around a little. He was all dressed up. He was a sissy. Then we started down toward the river and stood on the bank awhile, and I took hold of his collar and pushed him, but pulled him back again. I did that a couple of times, and then I gave him a shove and let him go in. He flopped around in the water for a while and then he went down.

Jimmy went with detectives to the riverbank near the University Bridge to point out the spot were the incident occurred. Once the boy was found, Jimmy's arraignment barely lasted a minute. He was held without bail and tried for murder.

During the trial, Dr. D. J. Davidson of the House of

Corrections claimed Jimmy was "impudent, rude, bullying and cruel" and added that he showed "no signs of remorse." At one point, when Jimmy left the witness stand, he picked up the Bible with which he had been sworn in and tried to walk away with it.

On July 2, Jimmy was committed to the Allentown State Institution for Mental Defectives. The municipal court psychiatrist concluded that the boy was legally sane and knew the difference between right and wrong but was a "congenital moral imbecile."

Jimmy remained in the Allentown hospital until June 1946, when, at 17, he was paroled. According to the hospital, he made an excellent rehabilitation and went on to "a good position" in some unnamed career.

Forming a
Blessed Union

1937

Although Ida Kunkel may have agreed politically with the sit-in strike against the J.C.J. Strahan hosiery mill in North Philly, she had to be less than pleased with the timing.

Her betrothed, Curtis Lees, was one of the twenty strikers.

Striking against hosiery plants was all the rage in Pennsylvania in the 1930s. The state's "Little New Deal," an offshoot of Roosevelt's National Plan, opened the doors for the CIO, which in turn led to increased union activity in Philadelphia. Among those striving toward full unionization were the American Federation of Full-Fashioned Hosiery Workers and the Amalgamated Clothing Workers of America, hence the lovebirds' dilemma.

But union activity was not going to keep those childhood sweethearts from forming an eternal bond. The June 1937 wedding went on as planned—but instead of the church aisle, the couple used the sidewalk in front of the Strahan plant, on Indiana Street.

146

Twenty-five policemen kept their eyes on the two hundred spectators while they, in turn, watched the bride, who wore white lace and carried white roses and snapdragons, walk the thirty-foot path from the curb. "Here Comes the Bride" was played on trumpet, saxophone, and accordion as she approached the groom at the factory entrance, which was decorated with two American flags and the CIO logo.

The twelve-minute service, difficult to hear because of passing trains, culminated in a kiss that was reported to have lasted exactly one second.

Following the ceremony, the new Mr. and Mrs. Lees took off immediately—for a distinctly unromantic visit to the Apex Hosiery Company plant at 5th and Luzerne, where 256 of Lee's brother unionists had been holding their ground since May 6. Following this show of solidarity, the couple hopped back in the limousine to a more traditional honeymoon site—Atlantic City.

The only damper on the celebration came not from scabs or strikebreakers but from the minister who conducted the service. In order to ensure that his good name would not be sullied by his association with the radicals, the Reverend Frank Duncombe of the Bala Cynwyd Methodist Episcopal Church passed out cards to state his position. He stressed:

> My coming here for this wedding has nothing to do with sit-down strikes. I am opposed to them. And I believe labor is making a serious mistake in opposing law and order. Sit-down strikes and the Ku Klux Klan are synonymous as they stir up class and race hatreds. I am against them.   ✴

147

Junker Jubilee

1938

In 1938 local dealers celebrated National Used Car Exchanges Week with a parade of twelve hundred used cars up Broad Street to help spur sales.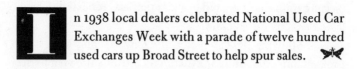

The 230 Fingers of
Dr. K
1938

Beethoven, it is said, always wished that someday
a musician would be able to take his sonatas and
perform them in such a way that they would sound
like a piano symphony.

Why he said that is not known.

But throughout the years, a number of visionaries
tried to fulfill Beethoven's dream without apparent success.
These included composer Carl Czerny, a contemporary of
Beethoven's, as well as the more recent but equally obscure
Percy Grainger, Walter Damrosch, and Eugene Goossens.

It took Dr. Carle Knisley, an Australian-born conductor, and a gang of Philadelphia women to finally bring this
musical daydream to life.

Knisley, a prominent music lecturer and writer, toyed
for years with the number of pianos and players necessary to
get the proper musical effect. He began with eight, but soon
upped the number. Theory turned to reality when, in 1938, he
recruited a group of female pianists (all in their late teens and
early twenties) and formed the Philadelphia Piano Orchestra.

Why only women? According to the maestro:

> They're more cooperative, more sensitive, they have
> a better ear for tone and volume than men . . . and
> besides, they look more decorative on the stage.

The women were mostly moonlighters. They included a sheet music saleswoman from Kresge's department store, a swimming teacher, a social worker, and a secretary.

The Philadelphia Piano Orchestra set up rehearsal space in an abandoned Swedish restaurant on Rittenhouse Square and later in its own Walnut Street studio. The arrangements were by Maestro Knisley himself, and the selection of pieces included such familiar works as "The Blue Danube," "Grand Canyon Suite," and "Tales from the Vienna Woods." The size of the group varied, but at its peak, it featured twelve pianos played at one time by twenty-three pianists.

Throughout the 1940s, the ensemble was a mainstay at the Met, Town Hall, and the Academy of Music. And although its scheduled South American tour was canceled due to wartime restrictions, it did tour America in 1949, making stops in Salina, Kansas, and Baton Rouge, Louisiana.

Throughout the ensemble's existence, the critics were polite, appreciating the precision and admiring the effort but conceding that the effect was less than stunning. "It must be admitted," said one scribe, "that the potentialities are not unlimited." Another noted that nothing can be done on more than two pianos that can't be done on one. "The Philadelphia Piano Orchestra," he wrote, "didn't refute the saying. But it made a brave effort." ✺

Arsenic and Old Philadelphia

1939

Carina Favato had been in court before. In 1936 she was a key witness in the trail of Bridget Caprara, who was accused of being a witch in violation of an 1861 act regulating fortune telling and soothsaying.

Favato had given Caprara $1,300 over sixteen months and $5,000 over ten years to cure her ailments and bring her better luck. "But I am sick yet," she testified, "And I have no good luck. And my boys, they get jobs . . . one, two days . . . they get laid off!"

Favato was also upset about the ground bones "the Witch" had given her. Apparently, they disappeared from her home on Bouvier Street. Favato insisted:

> The Witch—she got them. We locked the house, but she took the shape of a black cat. In the night she came in. This morning I look—and the bones are gone.

Neighbors said that Caprara had a habit of wandering down to the cemetery every Tuesday and Thursday night, waving her arms and muttering. Police stated that, over thirteen years, she had been paid nearly $100,000 from people wanting her to act as middle-person with the powers of darkness. Thanks in large part to Favato's testimony, Caprara, "The Witch of Venango Street" was convicted of fraud.

When Favato returned to court three years later, though, it was not as a witness, but as the accused. The charges: poisoning her seventeen- year-old stepson, her common law husband, and the husband of another woman on trial. One thing all three victims had in common were life insurance policies naming Favato as beneficiary, to a tune of over $16,000.

They weren't alone. According to detectives, Favato was part of a ring that targeted women they thought would be interested in collecting insurance on their husbands. Detectives reported:

> Sometimes they would make love to the wife and suggest getting rid of the husband. If they succeeded, they would point out that there should be a business arrangement. The women always did the actual poisoning. . . . In instances where the wife was unwilling or afraid . . . she would introduce a member of the ring to her husband and the man would invite the husband out to dine frequently. Then he would put arsenic in the food.

Favato pleaded from her cell in Moyamensing Prison:

I do not know what arsenic is. How could I give

arsenic to anybody? We all helped ourselves from the same bowl, and poured our wine from the same pitcher.

The court found otherwise. Despite her pleas of innocents, evidence mounted that Favato was part of a ring led by fake faith healer Morris Bolber and spaghetti salesman Herman Petrillo and his brother Paul. Favato, a notorious baseball fan who is said to have put spells on visiting teams at Shibe Park, pleaded innocent, but as the evidence mounted in the first of the three trials, she changed her plea to guilty.

"Well, I may just as well go to the chair," she said, "what have I got to live for?"

In the end, the Petrillo brothers were executed and Bolber and Favato received life sentences although twice, in April 1939, she tried killing herself in her cell, first by strangling herself with a handkerchief, then by scratching her wrist with a pin. Guards stopped her both times. ✠

Cracking Down on
Pinball
1941

While a bonfire, supervised by police, raged at the city dump in South Philadelphia, consuming $20,000 worth of confiscated pinball machines, Captain Craig Ellis of the vice squad announced, "We are determined to break up the practice of storekeepers permitting boys to gamble on these machines."

Ellis had been seizing machines since early 1941, acting on a court ruling that a pinball game could be hauled off if its owner was observed paying a winner in cash or other prizes. Ellis and his crew of twenty-five took to their task with a vengeance, making hundreds of busts and using a giant van to haul the offending games out of bars and drugstores. Assistant City Solicitor James F. Ryan announced his hope to ban all pinball machines "except those with foolproof guarantees against gambling."

However, an earlier State Supreme Court ruling held that pinball machines were games of skill, not gambling devices, and so could not be banned outright. That precedent was challenged in a Philadelphia court in March of

154

1941. Police argued that pinball had become the most heavily patronized form of gambling in the city, earning three times as much as the numbers racket. During one session, a pair of pinball machines was brought into the courtroom and played by both Ryan and Ellis, while Judge Levinthal watched. "It's a sucker's game," concluded Ellis, who did not win any free games.

Counsel for the machine owners disputed the charge. "This is amusement," said one lawyer. "The police have no more right to seize these than they would to pounce on a pack of cards in a store."

After hearing the arguments and watching the game played, Judge Levinthal decided that pinball machines could be confiscated not only if gambling was witnessed but also if a machine had a device for canceling free games (machine owners who awarded cash prizes usually allowed no free games for the winners and would remove the credits from the machine). This ruling made it much easier for police, since witnesses were no longer necessary.

Ryan hailed the decision as sounding "the death-knell of the pinball business in Philadelphia," and before long police had seized more than four hundred machines. In February 1942, the Superior Court of Pennsylvania expanded the ban to include even pinball machines that paid winners in free games only, essentially outlawing pinball in Philadelphia.

The death of pinball, however, was only temporary. Early in 1943, the state superior court changed its mind, allowing pinball to continue anew its wicked seduction of teenagers with too much time (and change) to spare. ✄

The Philadelphia
Experiment

1943

The Loch Ness has its monster. The Himalayas have their abominable snowman. Bermuda has its triangle. And, Philadelphia has the Philadelphia Experiment, a bizarre story that, thanks to one "eyewitness," has survived since the 1940s.

The public first heard about the experiment in 1956, from a Washington auto-parts salesman named Morris K. Jessup. Jessup had written a book called *The Case for the UFO* and was touring to promote it. While on tour he received a letter from Carlos Miguel Allende, with a return address in New Kensington, Pennsylvania (although the postmark was for Gainesville, Texas). In the letter, Allende told Jessup to ease up with the antigravity talk. According to Allende, the United States Navy had already played around with such things. He claimed that one such experiment, in

Marshall Cavindish, *The Unexplained* (New York: Marshall Cavendish, 1986), p. 309. Alan Elliott, "Were the Allende Letters a College Prank?" *Pursuit*, April 1976, pp. 43–44. Robert Goerman, "Alias Carlos Allende," *Fate*, October 1979, pp. 69–75.

October 1943, led to a bizarre incident in which the navy accidentally teleported a destroyer, DE-173, from a Philadelphia dock to Newport, Virginia, and back again in minutes.

According to Allende, who claimed he was there at the time:

> I watched the air all around the ship . . . turn slightly darker than all the other air . . . I saw, after a few minutes, a foggy green mist arise like a thin cloud. I think this must have been a mist of atomic particles. I watched as [it] became rapidly invisible to human eyes. And yet the precise shape of the keel and underhull of that ship remained impressed into the ocean water.

Strange enough. But Allende asserted that those on board the destroyer had suffered horrible side effects. Specifically, crew members unexpectedly lapsed in and out of visibility. Many went mad.

The intrigued but skeptical Jessup wrote to Allende asking for evidence. More than six months later, a reply came from Allende, now calling himself Carl M. Allen. Allen told the same story but wrote that he could not remember any exact dates or names of other witnesses. Jessup let the matter drop, but not for long. A year later, still lecturing, Jessup was pulled back into the story when he was handed a copy of his own UFO book filled with annotation by three writers, who made repeated references to the Philadelphia Experiment. The handwriting of one was clearly Allende/ Allen.

In 1959, Jessup committed suicide.

A decade later, the Aerial Phenomena Research Association reported that Allende/Allen had stopped by their office in Arizona and claimed that the whole thing was a joke.

Charles Berlitz, the writer who helped get America worked up over his Bermuda Triangle theory about disappearance in the Atlantic Ocean, didn't buy the admission. In 1979 he co-authored a book called *The Philadelphia Experiment: Project Invisibility*. In it, he claimed that the invisibility experiment did happen and that surviving witnesses were being harassed into not talking about it. Among his sources was Carl Allen, who now recanted his confession. Allen remained elusive, though, leaving some to speculate that he represented an extraterrestrial power that took root on Earth centuries ago.

Not quite. Allen was actually born in Springdale, Pennsylvania, in 1925. Known as a master leg-puller, he once masqueraded as an antique expert, another time he masterfully feigned a heart attack. Reporter Robert A. Geerman of *Fate Magazine* (which regularly accepts UFOs and other paranormal activity) gained access to Allen's notes, which were wildly inconsistent, and wrote a book, *The Allende Dossier*, in which he debunked the whole Philadelphia Experiment story.

Said Goerman:

> If we are to believe Allen, our naval hierarchy abandoned sanity . . . by conducting an experiment of enormous importance in broad daylight using a

badly needed destroyer escort vessel which at that moment was supposed to be guarding a convoy of merchant supply ships from Axis torpedoes.

Allen was not thrilled with the book. He wrote a letter to Goerman saying he would:

LOVE to shoot you at first sight . . . with a 12-gauge shot-gun at a 5-foot range, be too delighted happy & in fact exultantly over-joyed . . . to blow your empty stupid head off.

A bad movie, released in 1984, fictionalized the Philadelphia Experiment even further. 🦋

The Almost
Integration of
Baseball
1943

During World War II, professional baseball, like other industries in America, was facing a serious manpower shortage. According to Bill Veeck, whose father owned the Chicago Cubs, "The only fellows left were aged, ancient, injured or 4-F."

It seemed the perfect time for integrating some players from the popular Negro League with those in the majors. Public attention was already focused on racism in baseball. Protests were being held in Boston and New York, with picketers outside Yankee Stadium carrying signs that read, "If We Can Stop Bullets, Why Not Balls?"

In 1947 Brooklyn Dodgers manager Branch Rickey made history by signing Jackie Robinson, the first black man in major league baseball.

But four years earlier, the Phillies were almost the first team to break the color barrier in baseball when Bill Veeck

160

had an idea. He began negotiations to buy the Phillies from owner Gerald Nugent, who was ready to get rid of his losing team. Then he quietly lined up Satchel Paige, Roy Campanella, and other Negro League stars to join the Phillies when the deal came through.

Veeck's motives probably had little to do with affirmative action. Throughout his career in baseball he was best known for his unusual promotional activities, including an exploding scoreboard, baseball clowns, and a midget pinch hitter.

Veeck later recalled:

> There was a suspicion that if I tried to buy the Phillies and load up with Negro players, I was grabbing for the quick and easy publicity stunt and for a quick and easy way to rebuild a hopeless team. I am not going to suggest that I was innocent.

The first half of the plan went fine, with talks going smoothly between Veeck and Nugent. And perhaps history would have been made if Veeck had kept his plan quiet. "I had a plan where I was going to take the Phillies from seventh place to a pennant in one year. But the league got wind of my plan."

How did they find out? On his way back to his home in Chicago, Veeck stopped at the New York office of baseball commissioner Kenesaw Mountain Landis. During that visit, Veeck divulged his big plan to Landis's undoubtedly horrified ears. Landis never publicly admitted any non-integration policy, but his successor, Albert "Happy" Chandler, later noted that as long as Landis was in charge, "There weren't going to be any black boys in the league."

And so when Veeck arrived in Chicago the morning after the cordial meeting, he discovered that overnight the Phillies had been sold to the National League itself. Even worse, the sale was for half the price that Veeck was willing to pay. The move effectively kept black ballplayers out of baseball until 1947 and kept colorful Bill Veeck, who died in January 1986, out of Philadelphia sports forever. ✄

The Twisted
Tale of Slinky
1945

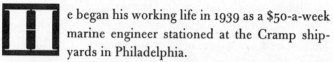

H e began his working life in 1939 as a $50-a-week marine engineer stationed at the Cramp shipyards in Philadelphia.

When he died in 1974, he was an evangelist and Bible salesman in Bolivia.

What connected these two divergent lives was an eleven-ounce coiled spring that his wife nicknamed Slinky.

Richard James was at sea one day when he observed a torsion spring (one with no compression or tension) fall off a table. He found himself watching the simple spring do amazing tricks as it rattled around on deck.

He rushed it home to his wife, telling her, "I think there could be a toy in this." He was right. With a $500 loan and the help of his wife, Betty, he ran tests, experimented with materials, and produced four hundred of the toys.

On a stormy night in November 1945, the couple, through a special arrangement with Gimbels department store in Center City, was allowed to set up an inclined plane in the toy department and demonstrate the spring's battery-less walking abilities. Within an hour and a half they were sold out.

Demand grew. By 1948 they had built a factory in Clifton Heights, Delaware County. In 1951, with sales still growing, they moved the plant to Paoli. By that time, subsidiary manufacturing was going on all over the world and Slinky was being sold in twenty countries. Published reports indicated that James Industries, with Richard as president and Betty as secretary-treasurer, had made the couple millionaires.

But developing one of the most popular toys in history was not enough for Richard. In 1960, seized by religious zeal, he resigned from the company, turned his stock over to his children, and left his wife. He moved to Bolivia, where he worked building printing presses for a Bible publisher. He founded a home for orphans and preached, in addition to developing a process for producing aluminum wire from ore. He also married again.

He visited his confused first wife and the children a few times to try to convince them that the Slinky business was not the road to heaven. But Betty wanted no part of her husband's new life.

After some rough times on her own, including a drop in sales that forced the sale of the Paoli plant, Betty got the company back on its feet. She moved the business to Hollidaysburg, near Altoona, and built a new plant for James Industries toys, including construction sets and pinwheels.

But the original metal Slinky is still the top seller. Betty can't even estimate how many have been sold since the Gimbels demonstration in 1945. "Until our 25th year, I thought Slinky was a novelty. . . . I honestly don't see what the attraction is." ✹

The Catch

1945

At Shibe Park on June 11, 1945, Bill Taylor, a.k.a. Ian Brokaw caught a baseball shot from a French 75-mm cannon while 30,000 spectators watched. The stunt was created as part of a war bond sales drive event that netted $5 million.

The thirty-year-old Taylor agreed to the stunt, provided there was no pre-event use of his name. He didn't want to worry his wife. 🦋

A Bitter Butter Battle

1947

ou are now leaving Maryland," said one sign at the Pennsylvania border. "Stock Up Here!"

In the 1940s, when Philadelphians smuggled contraband across state lines, they weren't just dealing in alcohol and firecrackers. They were also smuggling yellow margarine.

Nationally, the dairy lobby had been successful in keeping a tax levied on margarine since 1902, elevating its price to near that of butter. But in Pennsylvania and a handful of other states, there was more than just a tax—there was an outright ban on selling the spread.

Philadelphia dairy farmers were pleased with the ban, but others protested. Charles Von Tagen, executive secretary of the Grocers' Association, pleaded:

> People at last have awakened to the fact that oleo is not a substitute for butter, but a wholesome, nutritious, competitive product. We feel there is no more reason for a tax on oleo than there would be for one on string beans, spinach, coffee—or butter.

166

But the state government turned a deaf ear. In 1947, Senator Louis H. Farrell (R-Philadelphia) introduced a bill that would permit the unrestricted sale of margarine. A compromise bill was substituted, calling for grocers to pay an annual $5 fee to sell oleo. The fighting continued even after the federal tax was lifted in 1950. Philadelphians still had to cross borders to get the stuff.

It was not until August of 1951 that the state Senate Agricultural Committee in Harrisburg approved the Kessler Bill, which legalized the sale of yellow margarine in Pennsylvania. It was the tenth margarine bill to be discussed during that legislative session. "I would like the record to show there is nothing sinister, dishonest or corrupt about this bill," said cosponsor George E. Goodling (R-York). Later that month, it was signed into law by Governor John S. Fine.

As the bill was signed, cabs were lined up in Haddonfield, New Jersey, ready to ship cartons of margarine to Philadelphia from a Kraft Foods distribution point. The only complaint heard from grocers was that they were stuck with uncolored margarine, which had been legal, but was now unwanted. 🦋

All Hail the
Warrior Cabbies
1947

Free taxi service.

That's what was offered by a fleet of maroon-bodied, yellow-topped Fords lining the east side of City Hall on November 16, 1946. Each new taxi had a replica of a u.s. military discharge emblem on the roof light. It was a bold strategy in a losing battle.

It all started innocently enough. A group of World War II veterans banded together that year in a business venture to provide a much needed service to the city.

But when the proposal reached the Public Utilities Commission (puc) for approval, Yellow Cab Company protested, claiming that its service adequately met the needs of Philadelphians. The vets countered that Yellow Cab held an unfair monopoly. The fight raged both in and out of the hearing room. Vet-owned taxicabs were smeared with paint, their spark plugs were destroyed, and drivers were forced out of their cars.

Those tactics led the vets to make their unusual pitch to the public: free cab service.

168

The vets lost the first round. But they did not give up.

After being barred from operating cabs in the city streets in March 1947, the would-be cabbies turned their taxis into traveling fruit stands.

"How much?" a potential customer asked, interested in the bananas on the hood.

"Whatever you want to give," answered the driver. "We want this money to keep our fight going."

In April 1947 the fight continued with a PUC hearing, using veteran cabby Max Aizen as a test case. Sixty-four other applications waited in the wings. Attorneys for Aizen set out to prove that Yellow Cab was doing an inadequate job of handling the needs of customers. Disgruntled witnesses paraded before the commission, including a Germantown man who claimed he had great difficulty in getting taxis on rainy days, a professional entertainer who ordered a taxicab by telephone and, because of its lateness, lost a job, and a South Philadelphia man who claimed that a cabdriver declined to take him and his baby to the hospital until after the driver had eaten.

Yellow Cab had its own expert witnesses. Representatives of the Ritz-Carlton Hotel, the Forrest Theatre, the Rittenhouse Club, and dozens of others testified that they had no trouble hailing transportation.

On February 3, 1948, the PUC denied Max Aizen his cab license. Writing for the majority, PUC chairman John Siggins, Jr., stated what city cab customers have felt ever since: "Adequacy is a relative term." ✖

Boys Will Be Girls

1949

merica's Outstanding Lady Magician and the Only Lady Fire-Eater in the World." So went the billing for Donna Delbert, one of the strangest novelty acts on the music-hall circuit in England. Magic, at that time, was the realm of boys, with women usually serving as the disappearable, cut-in-half-able, barely clad sidekicks. Had Donna Delbert merely been a woman who made a living doing magic in theaters, that alone would have assured her a place in the history of magic.

But Donna Delbert had more of a story than that.

It was just after World War II, a time of celebration when people didn't ask too many questions. If they did, they would have realized that Donna Delbert didn't have much of a past. Her history went back only to the war. A little digging (which was finally done in a 1949 court martial) would have revealed that her name was actually Delbert Hill, and

"GI, 'Lady' Fire Eater Jailed for Desertion," *New York Times*, June 11, 1949. Teller, "My Search for Donna Delbert," *New York Times Magazine*, April 24, 1994, pp. 44–50.

she—actually, he—was a Philadelphia soldier who was AWOL from the United States Air Force.

While still exclusively wearing men's clothing, Hill served as an entertainer with the Air Force Special Service and had gotten some attention when, during an air raid in London, he continued performing his fire-eating act to keep the children in the audience from panicking. Such heroism led him to be part of a Fourth of July command performance for the Queen. But his rashness got in the way of fame. After being reassigned to latrine orderly duty, Hill got angry, got drunk, and went AWOL.

He resurfaced shortly thereafter, in a dress, as Donna Delbert, claiming to be the wife of a gunner killed at Normandy. For four years, wearing women's clothing and a wig, he displayed his magical talents on tour and managed to stay undiscovered—even when the magic business was slow and he had to take a job packing tobacco. Some thought he was a lesbian.

Said one girlfriend, who was privy to the truth:

> Always in public he wore his long, black hair in smart feminine styles, but when we were on our own, he would fasten back his locks with an elastic band and sometimes even pencil in a moustache. It was only when we had a lovers' quarrel that he used his normal, deep man's voice. Other girls never guessed.

It was that same woman, identified only as Betty, who discovered that Delbert was Donna and turned him in. At the time of his arrest, he was wearing his own hair very long and was, according to the press, "fully attired in woman's clothing."

The U.S. Air Force was not amused. They cut his curls and gave him two years of hard labor, with time out for prison talent shows. Upon his release, Delbert wrote to many of the people who had befriended Donna and confessed the truth. The responses were almost universally friendly. "You will be sure of a warm welcome whether you come as Donna Delbert or Private Hill," said one.

In 1952 Delbert Hill was back in Philadelphia, performing magic—in various costumes—for men's groups, Boy Scout troops, and mental institutions. In 1991 he was found dead, at 77, surrounded by the memorabilia of his, if not brilliant, at least very unusual, career. ❧

The Archaeology
Game

1950

Elsewhere in the world, such television game shows as "Beat the Clock" and "Break the Bank" were scoring high ratings and helping create what would one day be called "couch potatoes."

In Philadelphia, game show contestants may not have gotten anywhere near $64,000 for answering a question, but they did create one of the most esoteric, interesting, and odd programs ever to hit the airwaves.

The show, called "What in the World?" first aired in April 1950 on WCAU-TV. Host Froelich Rainey had no previous hosting experience, but he did have credentials of another kind. As curator of the University of Pennsylvania's Museum of Archaeology and Anthropology, he was eminently

Percy C. Madeira, Jr., *Men in Search of Man; The First Seventy-Five Years of the University Museum of the University of Pennsylvania*, (Philadelphia: University of Pennsylvania, 1964), pp. 59–60. " 'What in World' Is Now in Its 11th Year," *West Chester Local*, December 9, 1961. "TV Review: What in the World?" *New York Herald Tribune*, April 12, 1963.

qualified to direct the first—and the last—television game show centered on archaeology.

The structure was simple. A group of eminent scholars, like physical anthropologist Dr. Carleton Coon, sculptor Jacques Lipschitz, and Dr. Perry Rathbone, director of the Boston Museum of Fine Arts, made up the panel. These scholars would be presented with an item from either the university museum storeroom, from another museum, or directly from an archaeological site. Using their knowledge and powers of deduction, the scholars had to identify where the object was made, by whom, how old it was, and, perhaps most importantly, what the hell the damn thing was used for. None of the contestants received prizes, not even parting gifts, for their efforts.

For the viewers at home, who wouldn't know a hasanlu bronze if it knocked on their door, an offstage voice gave the answer prior to the on-camera appraisal.

After identifying the object, which the panel was able to do more often than not, there was a general discussion of the item and its place in history, complete with film clips and maps.

"What in the World?" was not as stodgy as it may sound. The show had its share of bloopers, most notably when Dr. Coon looked at a figurine and asked "Who's this wench?"

It was the Virgin Mary.

To liven up the festivities, the producers decided to try inviting audience members to send in items for expert identification. One piece of pottery fell to the floor and shattered before it could be identified. Most were identified as junk.

But the oddest thing about the show was its longevity. "What in the World?" aired nationally until 1955. ❧

A Visitor in
Fairmount Park
1953

The slogan for Philadelphia's celebration of the Constitution's birthday was the catchy "Miracle in Philadelphia." But there was, according to some, an actual miracle here, one that took place not on paper in 1787 but in a bush on the edge of Fairmount Park in 1953.

In that year, three girls from St. Gregory's Parochial School were watching some boys playing football in a field near 51st and Parkside. One of the girls reported:

> Suddenly I felt someone else by my side. A haze of light smoke enveloped the bush. . . . Suddenly the Blessed Virgin Mary appeared brightly illuminated through the cloud-like smoky haze.

The next afternoon the girls returned, armed with rosaries and two more friends. This time the experience was even more intense. One of the witnesses recounted:

> The Blessed Mother came right at us. . . . She had on a white gown and blue veil. She was life-sized.

175

Word spread rapidly, and the story was taken seriously by thousands, who came to the park to pay their respects, leave gifts, and see the manifestation.

The largest crowd came on October 25, when rumors circulated that another miraculous visit would occur. According to estimates by park officials, nearly fifty thousand of the faithful showed up to witness the event. A line of people stretched five hundred feet across the field. One merchant advertised candles, vigil lights, hot coffee, and chocolate. "I bet we served more than two thousand people today," bragged one restaurateur.

Wrapped around the tree and scattered on the ground were piles of articles, religious and otherwise, left by the faithful. These included rosaries, crutches, flowers, and orthopedic shoes. Mixed in was money totaling over $6,000.

Rumors circulated through the park that three miracles would be performed on that day, or that the first girl who had witnessed the vision would be transported to heaven. But the crowd left without seeing any blessed event. Some blamed it on "too many disbelievers." One man said he saw a figure in the trees, "but it was just the way the branches looked against the sky." The faithful continued to come after that day, but the crowds tapered off as months went by. The city finally decided to use the money left on the site to build a stone and wood shelter.

A recent trip to the area found the shelter still there, although covered now with graffiti (including the words "Welcome Home Wilber '85" in red spray paint). The bush was still budding, and on one low branch was hung an aqua and yellow plastic rosary. ✴

How the West
Was Shot
1953

L ive from the lot just behind WCAU's studios on Monument Road came "Action in the Afternoon," television's first and only live, daily half-hour western.

"Action in the Afternoon," the self-proclaimed "experiment in outdoor adventure," premiered February 2, 1953. The brainchild of WCAU programming director Charlie Vanda, the show transported viewers to the fictitious town of Huberle (taken from the names of network execs Hub Robinson and Harry Ammerle, who originally gave the OK to the project). All the Western archetypes were on hand: the peace-loving sheriff, the bad guys in black hats, and the pretty saloonkeeper (who, prior to the premiere, had been a WCAU secretary).

The Action crew soon learned the difficulty of shooting live in the great outdoors. Horses refused to give chase when the bad guys ran. Instead, they bit the microphones. At the drop of a ten-gallon hat, extra music had to be piped in to drown out City Avenue traffic. A runaway stagecoach collided with a parked car.

And to make matters even more difficult, the interior set was inside the studio, a good fifty-yard dash from the Main Street, Huberle, lot. When a cowboy pushed his way through the swinging doors of the saloon, the crew had to cut away to other characters while the actor sprinted to the set, caught his breath, and entered the beer hall.

The pesky critics nitpicked about things like "unconscious" bodies that moved, the questionable presence of forty-eight-star flags in the 1880s, and the occasional Philadelphia Eagles jacket that an actor would forget to take off before "action" was called.

Executive Director Leslie Urbach stood behind his show:

> Our stories have to be much better than those used in run-of-the-mill Hollywood westerns. In the movies, whenever the story goes sour, they just turn the cameras on the rocks and send in the good guys. Then they send in the same actors, with different hats, as the baddies. We don't have that privilege. We can't throw chases to take your mind off the story we haven't got.

"Action in the Afternoon" rode off into the sunset on February 9, 1954, barely a year after its premiere. The hero moseyed back to nightclub comedy. The saloonkeeper got hitched. And the sheriff returned to off-Broadway.   ✺

Rizzo Goes to Blaze's (Maybe)

1954

In 1954, a twenty-one-year-old West Virginia farm girl named Blaze Starr was all the rage on the stripping circuit. Why? Well, for one thing, her unique act included a live Asiatic black panther that removed her clothes by searching for small pieces of meat hidden there. It was not a subtle medium.

Philadelphia was one of her most popular stops, especially after May, when she was arrested at Steve Brodie's Show-Bar. Starr won her legal fight, the charges were dropped, and she continued for another forty weeks, but this time at the Black Cat Cafe on South Fifteenth Street, which happened to be in the district of police officer and yet-to-be-mayor Frank Rizzo. She was arrested there, too.

This time the charges had to do with what Starr and her feline assistant were doing on stage. The police called it "obscene," Starr preferred the term "interpretive." The judge, Samuel Clark, Jr., had trouble making up his mind.

Eventually he, too, threw out the charges. Starr moved on and the city thought it had heard the last of her. It was wrong. Two decades later, Starr wrote her autobiography. Much of the book dealt with her affair with Louisiana Governor Huey Long. But he wasn't the only prominent official mention. She also hinted strongly at a dalliance with Rizzo, who had since become Philadelphia's best known mayor.

To back up her claim, her publisher hired a polygrapher to give the ex-stripper, now author, a lie detector test. She easily passed it. Rizzo's response to the claims in the book:

> I will not dignify these outrageous charges by a response.

Crocketts on Parade

1955

In 1955, one hundred and fifty coonskin-capped kids dressed as their hero, Davy Crockett. The children circled City Hall and then proceeded down Market Street to Gimbels department store.

The Striking Case of
Lou the Barber

1955

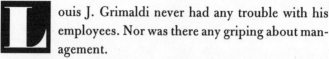

L ouis J. Grimaldi never had any trouble with his employees. Nor was there any griping about management.

So why did his business become the site of one of the city's stranger union confrontations?

Grimaldi's establishment was a one-man barbershop in Southwest Philly, and so unionization was the furthest thing from his mind. In 1955, when representatives of Local 9 of the Journeyman Barbers, Hairdressers and Cosmetologists Union asked him to join their brotherhood, Grimaldi said no. It seemed like common sense. Whenever he needed a raise, he pointed out, he could easily give it to himself without negotiation. When he wanted to leave work early, he gave himself permission.

But Grimaldi's "no" was unacceptable to Local 9. Soon, a cream-colored Cadillac pulled up in front of the barbershop with the first load of pickets. Business at the tiny clip joint immediately began suffering. Not only were customers scared away, but suppliers refused to deliver towels.

Grimaldi was confused, but he was not going to back down. He was, after all, the secretary of the Pennsylvania League of Master Barbers. He found a lawyer and took the case to court, where an injunction was granted keeping the protesters away from Grimaldi's door.

But the union would not back down. They appealed the decision and the case dragged on. By April 1959 it had reached the state supreme court.

What argument could the union possibly make? "The mere fact that he owns the barbershop doesn't give him the right to run the establishment in a way which adversely affects the working conditions of employees in other shops," argued Louis H. Wilderman, attorney for the union. Wilderman noted that Grimaldi's actions hurt union shops because the lone barber could keep his place open later than union rules allowed.

Not everyone was impressed by this line of attack. "Isn't this free America," asked one of the seven judges on the court. "Is there any freedom left?"

"There is also freedom of a union to picket peacefully and communicate its idea," Wilderman retorted.

The union arguments proved fruitless. Using lame literary imagery, Judge Michael A. Musmanno, writing for the unanimous court, held up Grimaldi's right to cut hair in the manner to which he had grown accustomed. "He has as much undisputed control over his barbershop as Robinson Crusoe had over his island on the Thursday before Friday arrived," he wrote.

The judge also noted that one of the primary issues

for unions was wages. And clearly it would be unusual for Grimaldi to ask himself for a raise, just as it would be silly to picket his own business should the union decide to go on strike. Other issues such as working conditions, benefits, and vacation time were equally absurd for the owner/operator.

Later that year, the U.S. Supreme Court, refusing to hear the case, let the decision stand. Said Grimaldi after the verdict:

I haven't won anything, so to speak.   🦋

The Neck Goes Down

1955

When a rookie joined the Philadelphia police
force in the early 1950s, it was common practice to initiate him by sending the officer down
to "the Neck" to do an inspection for housing violations.
Hours later, the exhausted and confused officer would return to headquarters to face the ridicule of fellow officers.

What was so bad about the Neck?

At its final official inspection, in May of 1955, Philadelphia's southernmost neighborhood, a thin strip of land
between Oregon and Pattison Avenues east of Third Street,
contained 97 houses, 173 adults, 74 children, 20 goats, and
809 ordinance violations.

The Neck (or Squatterville) was a neighborhood of
contradictions. Homes that had cars in front and antennas
on the roofs had no sewers. Some of the same residents who
went to Florida in the winter still relied on free water piped
in from fire hydrants. The neighborhood's main street was
called Stone House Lane, even though there had never been
a stone house anywhere near.

Said one longtime Squatterville man to a reporter:

> Look, friend, we've had inspectors here by the gross.
> Sometimes we talked to 'em. Other times we chased
> 'em. Either way, we knew nothing would ever come
> of it.

For a while, he was right. The area had been occupied by squatters since 1781. The only major cleanup occurred during the Depression, when the population of the Neck rose dramatically as the economy plummeted. Police moved in and cleared out the newly built shacks and lean-tos, but they left alone "established" Squatterville residents, those who had been living there for generations.

But what city officials failed to do in the past, big business, bad luck, and nature managed to do in 1955. That year a disastrous house fire on Stone House Lane killed four children and brought citywide attention to the gross violations of the housing code. A flood caused by a burst dike made many of the homes uninhabitable. Finally, plans for industrial development in the area and for a highway leading to the soon-to-be-built Walt Whitman Bridge made it only a matter of time before the neighborhood was gone.

In 1955 the Neck gave up. Residents were forced by the city to leave, and to make sure they stayed away, their houses were leveled. Said a longshoreman spending time at a local hangout, Sonny Smith's Luncheonette:

> We always chased away those pests who tried to
> dispossess us. But what can you do against a
> bulldozer? ✄

186

Mr. Clark Goes to
Washington
1960

I n 1952 "American Bandstand," hosted by WFIL radio DJ Bob Horn, made its television debut. The show, with its mix of youth-oriented music and real-life kids as dancers, proved popular for five years, until Horn was charged with statutory rape.

To replace him, the producers brought in another WFIL announcer, Dick Clark. In his Philadelphia record-spinning days, Clark, by his own admission, didn't pass up many money-making opportunities. He owned interest in at least three music publishing companies, a record presser, three record manufacturers, a management company, and a distribution outfit. It was not surprising that songs Clark had an interest in found their way onto his local dance show, "American Bandstand," boosting their popularity and adding to Clark's bank account.

Then "American Bandstand" went national. Despite *Billboard* magazine's impression—"If this is the wholesome answer to the detractors of rock-'n'-roll bring on the rotating pelvises,"—the show became even more popular. But with "American Bandstand" available nationwide, ABC became nervous and ordered Clark to either dump these interests or leave the show. Clark divested, the news went public and the Justice Department took an interest. Soon the House subcommittee investigating alleged fixing on television game shows decided to expand its scope to include payola and other unsavory broadcast practices.

And so, in April 1960, Mr. Clark went to Washington and faced the music.

Some subcommittee members missed the point, asking Clark why he never played Perry Como or Frankie Laine on his show. Others asked about more serious matters. One witness had tabulated that Clark owned a share in nearly 30 percent of the records played on the show. In addition, the average Clark-invested tune had a "Bandstand" lifespan of 7.8 weeks, while the others lasted only 4.7 weeks. This surprised Clark: "Maybe I did so without realizing it," he sheepishly admitted.

More evidence surfaced. Clark had received a ring, a necklace, and a fur stole from a producer. Said Clark: "We kept them because it was difficult under the circumstances to do otherwise."

A songwriter gave Clark a 25 percent royalty on a song worth $7,000. Said Clark: "I told him that the payment wasn't necessary. His answer was that he had made a promise and that he intended to fulfill his promise and did."

Clark also admitted that one of his companies was bribing local DJs for airplay. Said Clark: "I would no more think of telling Harry Chipetz [his partner in the company] how to run his business than the man in the moon."

ABC claimed they had already investigated Clark and concluded with "faith and confidence in Dick Clark's integrity." Yet it was later shown that the affidavit the network asked Clark to sign was not the same as that given to other DJs.

Notorious Cleveland DJ Alan Freed, who was fired for accepting payola, testified that if he had had to sign the same affidavit Clark signed, he would have gotten away "clean as snow."

Yet, in the end, the subcommittee could find nothing illegal in the activities that made Clark a millionaire. "Obviously," concluded subcommittee chairman Oren Harris, "you're a fine young man."

"An Insult to Sex"
1961

crass example of filth and a cesspool of corruption," thundered Montgomery County District Attorney Harold W. Spencer. "A danger to the welfare of the community," added Philadelphia D.A. James C. Crumlish, Jr.

By 1961, when Spencer issued a warning that booksellers in his county would be arrested if they continued to sell it, Henry Miller's novel *Tropic of Cancer* was already twenty-eight years old. But Crumlish waited until after his November re-election to pounce. After two police officers purchased the book in Center City, the D.A. sought a temporary injunction against the seller, Robin's Book Store. At the hearing, Assistant D.A. Arlen Specter called the book "filthy trash," Common Pleas Court Judge Vincent A. Carroll called it "literary smut," and the injunction against the book was granted.

The judge's decision had its desired effect. *Tropic of Cancer*, a huge seller in its ninety-five-cent paperback edition, disappeared from store shelves in Philadelphia. Curious readers turned to the Free Library, but so did Crumlish, who suggested to Library Director Emerson Greenaway that the book be removed from circulation. Greenaway argued that the eighty-six copies in the various branches were designated only for readers nineteen and older. But Judge Carroll fretted over all those impressionable people between nineteen and twenty-one. Greenaway gave in (under threat of prosecution) and instructed all borrowers to return the copies to the nearest branch. Two weeks after the Free Library ban, the University of Pennsylvania and Temple University removed copies from their libraries. A spokesperson for Drexel said the school's single copy had disappeared, but if it ever turned up, it would be suspended from circulation.

In the meantime, Crumlish pushed for a permanent injunction against Robin's. The trial was highlighted by the testimony of Dr. Austin Joseph App, a LaSalle English professor. App called Miller a fornicator, an adulterer, and a thief, and said that people who spoke such words as those in the book were "swine . . . that's what we called them in the Army."

Penn professor Dr. E. Scully Bradley, a witness for the defense, had a different perspective. He said that he had been familiar with all the four-letter words in the book by the time he was fifteen years old and hadn't been corrupted.

In April of 1962, Judge Carroll ruled that the book catered to prurient interests and was therefore obscene. He also complained that the novel had "no character development, no story, no plot and no message" and that it was "an insult to sex."

Meanwhile, the Free Library's copies of the book had been reclassified as historic records and stored in the library vaults. They remained there even after the U.S. Supreme Court lifted its ban on the sale of the novel. Even then, though, dissenting justice Michael A. Musmanno got in some harsh words of his own, calling Henry Miller "moral public enemy number one."

Divine Intervention

1961

He was born in the South, as George Baker, although accounts differ as to exactly where. In 1915, inspired by preacher Samuel Morris, he moved to Brooklyn.

There, he founded a group that lived together, shared meals, and turned over all that they earned to "The Messenger," who happened to be Baker himself. Over a few years, The Messenger underwent a name change and became Major J. Divine, then Rev. J. Divine, then simply Father Divine (God). Throughout the growth of his church, he preached the need to turn over assets to God to become angels (who were given names such as Hozanna Love, Onward Universe, and Frank Incense). Celibacy was strictly enforced. Hundreds joined him when he moved his church to Harlem.

Robert Weisbrot, *Father Divine and the Struggle for Racial Equality*, (Champaign: University of Illinois Press, 1983), pp. 9–11, 216–219. Joseph Bulgatz, *Ponzi Schemes, Invaders from Mars and More Extraordinary Popular Delusions and the Madness of Crowds* (New York: Harmony Books, 1992), pp. 351–359. Robert Weisbrot, *Father Divine*. (New York: Chelsea House, 1992), pp. 104–113. "Remarks of Rev. James W. Jones, Pastor of People's Temple, Indianapolis, Indiana," *The New Day*, August 2, 1958, pp. 19–21.

Legal troubles led Father Divine to move from New York with a few hundred of his followers in 1942. According to biographer Robert Weisbrot:

> The years in Philadelphia . . . did not witness a revival of Divine's Peace Mission movement but rather its quiet consolidation. . . . During this period the once vital economic life of the Peace Mission waned.

But, just as Samuel Morris had inspired him, Divine inspired a new generation of preachers.

In 1961 James Warren Jones visited Philadelphia. Jones had been involved in his own religion almost from the womb. His mother believed she was the reincarnation of Mark Twain and that her son was the Messiah. He believed it too, and had claimed that he had also been the Egyptian pharaoh Ikhnaton, Buddha, and Lenin.

He led a growing church in Indianapolis that stressed service to the poor. But it wasn't until he met Father Divine that Reverend Jim Jones, leader of the People's Temple, found his inspiration.

After his visit to Philadelphia Jones said:

> I came and saw the reality of things that I had known for years . . . just at the very time when I could have given the whole thing up and become defeated. I came to the Peace Mission and gained new zeal and new power!

From then on, Jones insisted his followers call him

194

"Father" or "Dad," insisted all money from his members be turned over to him, and started calling his inner circle "Angels."

By 1978 Father Divine had long since died and his movement had quieted down. Jones, however, was on his way to infamy by leading a mass suicide of his followers in Guyana. Analyzed Weisbrot:

> Unlike Father Divine, his intended model, who combined a will to power with constructive purpose, Jones ultimately made power alone the center of his cult role. When that power, too, began to dissolve, there were no further supports to sustain his life or movement.   🦋

J. I. Rodale,
Hygiene Playwright
1961

One of the leading champions of healthy living in the 1900s was J. I. Rodale, founder of Allentown's Rodale Press. Fascinated by farming, Rodale moved to Allentown in 1930, just a few years before the electrical appliance maker was seeing the evils of factory-made fertilizers and synthetic insecticides. In 1942 he helped launch *Organic Farming and Gardening* and, in 1950, *Prevention* magazine.

David Armstrong and Elizabeth Metzger Armstrong, *The Great American Medicine Show: Being an Illustrated History of Hucksters, Healers, Health Evangelists, and Heroes from Plymouth Rock to the Present* (Englewood Cliffs, N.J., 1991), pp. 228–229. *Three Plays by J. I. Rodale* (Allentown, Penn.: J. I. Rodale, 1966). Suzanne Zelkowitz, "Curtain up, Light the Lights," *Folio*, August 1991. "Rodale Will Open Intimate Theatre," *New York Times*, January 13, 1952. "Busy 'Impudent Wolf' Dramatist Now Turns Energies to Musical," *New York Times*, November 20, 1965. "Theatre: ''Toinette' Opens," *New York Times*, November 21, 1961. "'Toinette' Sponsor Rebukes Its Critics," *New York Times*, November 28, 1961. "'Toinette' A New Musical Comedy: The Playwright vs. The Critics." (Advertisement) *New York Times*, November 28, 1961.

196

But keeping people healthy was not Rodale's only passion. He also wanted to be a playwright. Unlike most struggling artists, though, Rodale had his own bankroll to back himself up.

What was unusual about his theatrical ambitions, and what made Rodale unique among playwrights, was his choice of subjects—health.

His drama *The Goose*, which was built on the premise that deficient diet was a contributing factor in juvenile delinquency, inspired one critic to comment:

> It is supremely inept. It is magnificently foolish. It is sublimely, heroically, breathtakingly dreadful. It inspires a sacred terror. It is beyond criticism.

In 1961 his musical adaptation of Molière's medical satire *The Imaginary Invalid*, renamed *'Toinette*, provoked *New York Times* critic Howard Taubman to rant:

> There must be a lesson in a disaster like the witness, tasteless *'Toinette*, which was allowed into the Theatre Marquee last night . . . the author of the book [Rodale] should have to pay at least ten times the rates he would owe Molière if he were alive and his work were still covered by copyright.

Rodale took that one personally. He took out a lengthy advertisement in the *Times* the following week headlined "*'Toinette* a New Musical Comedy. The Playwright vs. the Critics." In the ad, Rodale wrote about the audiences being "hilarious in laughter and applause" and cited such odd sources as Phillip Fleet, health editor for Prentice-Hall publications, who said:

197

I, for one, would give *'Toinette* a rave notice. In my opinion, it is one of the most delightful musicals I have ever seen.

Rodale went on to describe how "indecent" and "vicious" the real critics were.

The critics had not reviewed *'Toinette.* They had reviewed J. I. Rodale, editor of *Prevention*, the largest circulating popular health magazine in the world, a magazine that because it is telling the truth is a menace to certain powerful medical and industrial interests. These people and their publicity agents are building me up as a menace, a quack, a food faddist.

But the *'Toinette* incident did not scare away Rodale. In 1962 Rodale went a step beyond most writers and producers. He used more than $100,000 to purchase his own theater in Manhattan, the Royale at 62 East Fourth Street.

He couldn't resist the similarity between his own surname and the name of the theater. He ordered the Y replaced with a D and it became the Rodale.

The stated purpose of the new theater was to present plays that were "helpful, beneficial and that teach something, and that tie in with character development, improvement and education" as well as ones that deal with "the facts of history, health, and interesting knowledge."

The plays—including a Little Red Riding Hood satire called *The Hairy Falsetto*—have drifted safely into the realm of the unrevived.   ✳

The Philadelphians
of Oz
1963

Most Americans think that Dorothy's adventures in Oz began with a twister and ended with a clicking of a pair of special shoes. But the girl from Kansas has racked up some serious frequent flyer miles coming and going to the Emerald City since L. Frank Baum's *The Wonderful Wizard of Oz* was first published back in 1900.

But whereas Baum founded and wrote the first fourteen Oz books, it was Philadelphian Ruth Plumly Thompson who directed most of the treks. After Baum died in 1919, Thompson, editor of the Sunday children's page for the *Philadelphia Public Ledger*, was approached by Baum's publishers to take over the wildly successful series. She took the assignment and produced an Oz book nearly every year, from 1921's *The Royal Book of Oz* (credited to Baum for continuities sake, but actually written by Thompson) through

Ruth Plumly Thompson, "An Ozian Television Odyssey," *The Baum Bugle*, Autumn 1991, p. 34.

Ozoplaning with the Wizard of Oz, which came out in 1939, the same year as the MGM movie version of Dorothy's first journey to the Emerald City.

By that year Thompson had grown tired of Oz and another Philadelphian, John R. Neil, took over. Yet until her death in 1991, Thompson was consistently called on by fans to comment on her books.

In 1963 such a call turned nasty.

On December 16, the seventy-two-year-old author was invited to participate in a Christmas special on WCAU-TV's "Ten Around Town" series. Her sister accompanied her to what promised to be an innocuous question-and-answer session in the station's Bala Cynwyd studio.

A set had been built featuring familiar Ozian images—a yellow brick road, Emerald City, the Scarecrow, the Tin Woodman, and the Cowardly Lion.

The interview went smoothly, and Thompson was happy with the banter with reporter Shyrlee Dallard. The problem arose when, in the last six minutes of the show, a surprise guest (at least to Thompson) was added to the show—a representative from the Philadelphia Free Library.

One would not normally assume that a librarian would be the enemy of an author of nineteen volumes in perhaps the most popular series of American children's books of this century, but there had been longstanding issues between librarians and Ozians and the 1960s were a particularly hostile time toward fantasy books.

Ruth Plumly Thompson described what happened:

Well, hell's bells! Laden with books, papers, and

200

a warlike expression, said lady strode on, launching into a disgraceful tirade. Facing the audience instead of me, she talked so fast I couldn't get in but a few outraged responses. The gist of her remarks was that children had to be guided in their reading as in their eating and not allowed to indulge in trash. . . . That was why the Free Library had a whole set of Oz books in the back for research and but only two on the shelves.

Thompson fought back vigorously and, when the taping was ended, the librarian stormed off.

After listening to sympathetic comments from the crew, Thompson went home exhausted. The phone rang shortly thereafter. It was the "Ten Around Town" director, asking if Thompson could come back the next day for a retaping, this time without the librarian.

Reported Thompson of the results:

The show came off on Christmas day and was really neat! While I was upset at my wan appearance, no one else seemed to notice it and telegrams, calls and letters have been coming in ever since. But I'll never go down the Yellow Brick Road again. At least not on television.   ✺

The Deb Rampage
1963

In 1963, a group of young, clean-cut upper-crust Philadelphians were featured prominently in an article in *Life* magazine, then one of the most popular publications in the country. But none of their parents were too proud.

THE HEADLINE: "A Wanamaker Debut Begins . . . And Ends in a Rampage."

THE SUBHEAD: "Young people's don't-give-a-damn attitude hits a new extreme."

The chaos took place on Long Island, when debutante Fernanda Wanamaker Wetherill of Chestnut Hill made her debut at Westerly, the Southampton estate of her mother and stepfather. The crowd numbered over eight hundred,

"30-Room Mansion Wrecked by Youths After Debut on L.I.," *New York Times*, September 4, 1963." "Affluent Delinquency," *New York Times*, September 5, 1963. "Judge on L.I. Scolds Officials for Laxity on Fracas at Debut," *New York Times*, September 13, 1963. "Suffolk May Indict Debut Ball Vandals," *New York Times*, September 22, 1963. "Two at L.I. Debut Testify on Brawl," *New York Times*, October 3, 1963. "Ball Is Canceled for L.I. Debutante," *New York Times*, November 3, 1968. "A Wanamaker Debut Begins . . . and Ends in a Rampage," *Life*, November 20, 1963.

and the supervised dance was similar to dozens of others that the young crowd had attended as each young lady ceremoniously entered adult society.

At 2 A.M., the tone shifted when the Meyer Davis orchestra was replaced by a rock band called the El Carls and the dancing grew more raucous. The summer home began to be littered by passed out bodies. Around 5 A.M., when the party was supposed to end, the partiers begged their hostess to keep the action going, but Fernanda Wanamaker Wetherill Leas, mother of the Deb, would only compromise. If they wanted to keep it up, they could go back to the Ladd house, a nearby mansion where Leas had set up beds and cots for seventy-five tired partygoers.

About a hundred of them, and the band, relocated to the ballroom of the Ladd house. A beer run led by Fernanda-the-younger's brother, Dring, gave new life to the debs and their dates.

As dawn approached, the games began. A ship's wheel over the fireplace (nobody said the wealthy all had taste) became a target for wall climbers. Guys formed a human pyramid to reach the chandelier. Furniture was taken out to the surf. Rocks crashed through the windows. The chandelier smashed to the floor. The siege on the house lasted past noon, when sleep began to overtake the home wreckers, and the house finally quieted down. Until the police arrived.

Long Island's finest showed up at the house at about 4 P.M., by which time most of the windows were broken and about a third of the kids were still on their feet. They were rounded up, photographed, and taken to the police station.

Deciding that some publicity was warranted, the chief gave the story to the newspapers. Local reporters spread the word until the affair was covered by the *New York Times*, *Life* magazine, all the hometown Philly papers, and even the *London Times*. Tom Wolfe, in his pre–*Right Stuff*, *Bonfire of the Vanities* days, wrote about it for the *New York Herald Tribune*. Johnny Carson joked about it.

Four Philadelphia kids were indicted, but the scale of the riot left it difficult to pin any specific acts on any specific suspects. Press coverage notwithstanding, the cases were ultimately dismissed for lack of evidence. ❧

The Lion's Tale
1964

When Harry Sautter, a former race car driver and current gas station owner, bought Leo from a New York animal importer for $250, he figured nobody would be bothered by the presence of a semi-invalid lion. And no one was, for two years at least. During that time, Sautter developed a strong bond with the beast. The duo became a common sight wrestling in Sautter's back yard and driving together—Leo rode shotgun—in Sautter's tow truck.

But not all thought the king of beasts was an appropriate house pet. On November 4 of 1964, Sautter's neighbors presented a petition signed by fifty-five local residents demanding something be done about the late night roaring and offensive smells coming from 2428 Welsh Road.

At first, it seemed like a loophole would save Leo. A quick look through the township ordinance revealed that there were laws banning chickens and pigs but nothing against lions. Still, township commissioners decreed that Sautter would have to get rid of Leo or face prosecution.

Sautter, by all accounts, could not quite make up his mind what to do. First he said he was going to fight the case in court. Then he said he would bow to the commissioners and give Leo away. Then he decided to have Leo's roar surgically removed, which he did, at the Veterinary Hospital of the University of Pennsylvania.

But the roar was only one detail in the legal fight. According to Public Safety Chairman John Gibson, "I still feel Willow Grove is no place for a lion."

Sautter said he would fight all the way to the U.S. Supreme Court and presented a counter petition signed by three hundred Abington-area residents in favor of the lion to a meeting of the public safety committee of the Abington Township Commissioners. For an hour and ten minutes, Sautter held the floor with talk of Leo's virtues. Sautter filibustered:

> He is the most docile lion in the world. I have to open four locks to get into his cage. . . . I don't take him in my tow truck anymore because he's too big. . . . I love my lion. I got him when he was two months old. I take better care of Leo than of myself.

Sautter also pointed out that several of the fifty-five who signed the original position were sorry that they had been talked into signing it.

The politicos were not impressed. A zoo curator stated he would not advise keeping a pet lion that was more than six months old in a private home. Chairman Gibson said a man from Quebec had written a letter detailing the case of a lion there who had killed a two-year-old child two weeks earlier. Said Sautter:

Just because one man kills somebody, you don't outlaw all people. So why should my lion go?

To Sautter's credit, twelve Girl Scouts showed up and said, "We're for the lion."

In early December an ordinance was passed at last making illegal "animals of the species which is generally of a wild nature." The new year brought with it an injunction against Sautter, but the gas pumper's lawyer countered with a technicality, stalling the process even further. The case was turned over to the county court, which was baffled.

Said Judge Frederick B. Smillie

How do you regulate the roar of a lion? . . . What if he wanted to keep five lions, even well-regulated? Could he also keep a cobra?

Leo won this one, with Montgomery County Judge Robert Honeyman dismissing the Abington Township complaint as unsubstantiated for lack of an allegation of nuisance, and gave the township twenty days to do the substantiating.

During that time, it looked like others in the animal kingdom were going to come to Leo's defense. Flame (a tiger), Frosty (a black panther), Ferd (a chimp), and Lemo (a seven-hundred-pound male lion) were scheduled to be shipped into the area in late March by Richard Lockwood, a publicity-seeking animal trainer from Unionville, Indiana. Lockwood agreed to split any money he made on promotions here with Sautter. "I'll stay as long as necessary to prove that all lions are not wild," said Lockwood.

But Sautter's lawyer nixed that idea. And Leo wasn't

really up for company. While the township was presenting expert testimony that Leo was both wild and a lion, Leo was being fed intravenously and not responding to medication. In early April, the buzz was that Leo, who hadn't been seen in weeks, was dead. Lawyer Hubert Yollin said, "I can neither confirm or deny the rumor."

He didn't need to. On April 12, Sautter let word out that the beast had an impacted bowel. Following that announcement, Police Chief Frank Jackson stopped by Sautter's home but was refused admission. The next day, two police officers with a search warrant and a camera proved that Leo was alive.

On April 20, despite testimony by Fred Ulmer of the Philadelphia Zoo ("He's crippled but he can be dangerous,") a justice of the peace threw out charges against Leo even after the township proved that Leo was a lion and wild. The township, said the justice of the peace, had failed to prove that Sautter was in persistent violation of the ordinance.

With the appeal pending in Montgomery County court, Leo died on the operating table at 9:45 on the evening of June 16. By then he had wasted away from acute constipation and had not eaten for two weeks. Dr. Daniel Bleicher, owner of Hamilton Animal Hospital in Roslyn, said death came as anesthesia was being administered as preparation for a last-minute operation to save his life. "We did everything we could," said Bleicher.

As for Sautter, he said he would continue to fight for resident's rights to own wild pets. Despite his loss, he was accepting of the reaper. "I'm glad it's all over," said Sautter. "I met many nice people." ✄

Room at the Top

1967

The National Hockey League was expanding, and some savvy businesspeople thought that Philadelphia should get on the bandwagon and house one of those expansion teams. But in order to land one, a city had to show that it had an arena that could house such a team. After all, there had not been a major indoor sports facility built in the city since the Civic Center in 1931.

The plan was to build a privately owned structure in the vast parking lot of the recently constructed Veterans Stadium. Mayor Tate loved the idea and ordered his people to cut as much red tape as possible to get the project moving. A few months later, Philadelphia landed one of the franchises, and the building developers faced a deadline: the structure had to be up and running in less than a year.

"11,000 Safe as Winds Rip Hole in Roof of Spectrum," *Philadelphia Inquirer*, February 18, 1968. "15-Man Crew Starts Repairs at Spectrum," *Philadelphia Inquirer*, February 19, 1968. "Wind Rips Hole in Spectrum Roof, 10,000 File out; Shows Canceled," *Philadelphia Bulletin*, February 18, 1968. Ed Snyder, "I Remember: The Day the Roof Blew off the Spectrum," *Philadelphia Magazine*, March 1989, pp. 29–30.

Ground was broken in June 1966. Miraculously, and through nearly round-the-clock work, the Spectrum was completed fifteen months later. It opened on September 30, 1967, with a performance by the Quaker City Jazz Festival. The next night, the second half of the jazz festival attracted 17,500 patrons, the largest indoor audience for anything in the history of Philadelphia.

Over the next few months, the newly formed Philadelphia Flyers hockey club was slowly building a following, arena attractions were booked, concerts were scheduled, heavyweight boxing champion and local hero Joe Frazier defeated challenger Tony Doyle, the Moscow Circus performed, and Mayor James H. J. Tate held his inaugural ball on the Spectrum floor.

The future looked bright.

And then, on February 17, 1968, the thirty-two-mile-per-hour winds howling through South Philadelphia, blew the roof off the Spectrum.

Not all of it, actually, just a hole fifty by one hundred feet. It happened just before 2 P.M. as 11,000 spectators sat waiting for the Ice Capades to begin on the ice below.

"It sounded like an airplane going over, then parts of the roof started falling in and the people started screaming," said an eyewitness. Nobody was hurt inside, but three people suffered minor injuries when they were hit by debris in the parking lot.

A short while later, Hal Freeman, president of the Spectrum, got on the PA system to calm the crowd. Not long after, the show was canceled, at a loss of more than $150,000. Back on the PA, Freeman announced:

210

It will be impossible to perform today. You can see the roof.

The band played "Off We Go into the Wild Blue Yonder" as the crowd, largely consisting of Boy and Girl Scouts, was ushered out.

While officials scratched their heads, the Philadelphia Flyers hit the road for an unplanned series of away games.

A representative of the roofing company said that it was probably the "airfoil" efftect that caused the damage. "Usually it is, when a roof goes off," he said. 🦋

Snowballs at Santa

1968

Admittedly, the half-time show on snow-covered Franklin Field was a bit of a disappointment, even to people who like such things. The band could not go out because of the field condition. A float created by Ed Zaberer's restaurant near Atlantic City proved too heavy for the field. All that was left was a man in a red suit who had to bring holiday joy to the grumpy fans.

It was December 15th, the Christmas game at which the Philadelphia Eagles faced off against the Minnesota Vikings. The snow had stopped just before game time and, as they usually are, things were more rowdy in the cheap seats. That's where, during the halftime show, one anonymous wise guy made Philadelphia sports fans famous across the country.

"Jingle Bells" played over the loudspeakers as Santa took a spirited walk out onto the field. He made it to about the thirty-five-yard line when the first projectile, a snowball tossed from the cheap seats, landed. By the time Santa made it to the fifty, the single toss turned into a barrage.

Bill Mullin, "Santa Claus Isn't Coming to this Town," *Philadelphia Magazine*, December 1990, pp. 31–34.

Santa knew where he wasn't wanted. He turned and retraced his steps to get out of the line of fire. At the twenty, he turned and shook his fist at the upper decks. It was Kris Kringle's last comment to the Phillies' fans. He left the field, changed out of his red suit, and went home. ✄

The Coxson Case
1973

ost politicians start out as officeholders and wind up getting arrested. I aim to reverse that process.

So said Major B. Coxson during his bid for the Camden mayoral office.

Coxson, a friend of Muhammad Ali, had a proud history of trouble. "I was elected president of Benjamin Franklin High School in Philadelphia when I was fifteen," he told one interviewer. "There were 2,200 students and I got 2,700 votes."

He was the proud owner of eleven Rolls-Royces and several Lincoln Continentals, Jaguars, and other custom-built vehicles. It was his love of automobiles that got him

"Camden Mayor Aspirant Fatally Shot on His Estate," *New York Times*, June 9, 1973. "U.S. Joining Inquiry on Jersey Slaying," *New York Times*, June 10, 1973. "People in Sports: Ali in Training, Not Hiding," *New York Times*, June 15, 1973. "Coxson is Buried with Pomp and Ceremony in Pennsylvania," *New York Times*, June 17, 1973. "FBI Seizes Suspect in Coxson Slaying," *New York Times*, June 29, 1973. "Jersey Will Try Coxson Suspect," *Times*, June 39, 1973. "Seven Are Indicted in Muslim Slayings at Home in Capital," *New York Times*, August 16, 1973.

into trouble. He was arrested seventeen times and convicted ten times on fraud and larceny charges. He served twenty-two months on charges of involvement in an interstate car-theft ring. When the IRS seized a pair of his cars, he retaliated by building a tandem bicycle and having his chauffeur cruise him through Camden.

His company, Continental Auto Wholesalers, was indicted in 1967 on conspiracy to steal from a check-cashing business using his car business. That case was still pending seven years later when he ran for mayor of Camden, losing to Angelo J. Erichetti. Coxson lived in Cherry Hill, New Jersey, with, according to the *New York Times*, no visible means of support and "with a great show of affluence in an area of $200,000 homes."

In June of that same year, 1973, Coxson was shot in his Cherry Hill home. His common law wife, Lois Robinson Luby, was also seriously wounded, along with two of her children (one fatally). A third child, thirteen-year-old Lex, escaped in his underwear, hands and legs bound by neckties. He hopped across the grounds to a neighbor's house where he banged his head against the glass and screamed until someone let him in. Coxson was found kneeling beside the bed, shot in the back of the head, dead.

Rumors circulated that the killers were also after Muhammad Ali, who was training in Deer Park, Pennsylvania, for his upcoming title fight with Ken Norton. Said Ali:

> There's only one contract out for me, and that belongs to Ken Norton for our fight, and I've got one out for him, too.

Federal investigators quickly linked the killings to Ronald Harvey, who was also wanted for slaying seven people in a Washington, D.C., Muslim headquarters owned by Kareem Abdul-Jabbar. Harvey, also known as 14-X, was arrested at his home in South Philadelphia. He was given seven life sentences for the Washington murders and two more for the Cherry Hill slayings. ✄

Buried Alive

1975

In October 24, 1975, a man identified only as handsome, in his twenties, a father of two, six foot three-and-one-half inches, and in the food business near Lancaster County, was buried in a self-made fiberglass coffin under a striped tent at 12th and Walnut Street.

For fifty cents, the curious could peek into a glass-covered tube and look at the very-much alive face of the bearded Phantom in his week-long home six feet underground. The coffin allowed him to move his head and little else for the week he would remain underground. Food, sent down another tube, was provided by a nearby deli. The biggest problem encountered, said his wife, "was the salad I dropped on his head." Said the rationalizing spouse to curious reporters:

> It really does take guts, you know. If there was any emergency, like appendicitis or something, it would take us a few hours to get him out. 🦋

"Young Phantom Lies 6 Feet Deep, But Not Asleep," *Philadelphia Bulletin*, October 28, 1975.

Silencing the
Candidates

1975

It was a major coup for Philadelphia. The first of the presidential debates between unelected half-term President Gerald R. Ford and his democratic challenger, Governor Jimmy Carter, would be held on the stage of the Walnut Street Theatre. A panel led by ABC news commentator Edwin Newman fired questions for eighty-one minutes on such topics as tax cuts, conservation, and nuclear safety. Then, while the nation looked on, Carter was asked to follow up on Ford's comments about government accountability. Said Carter:

> Well, one of the very serious things that happened in our government in recent years, and has continued up until now is a breakdown in the trust among our people in the . . .

Silence.

Ninety million people gave a collective "huh" as Carter

"Sound Is off Air for 27 Minutes," *New York Times*, September 24, 1975.

continued speaking but nothing was heard. The audience in the theater was baffled. Stagehands shouted. Technicians scrambled for answers.

"Excuse me, Governor," said Newman to the still speaking Carter, "I regret to have to tell you that we have no sound going out on the air."

Thus, the candidates had to face one of the greatest tests that any candidates have ever had to face—looking presidential, for twenty-seven minutes, without saying a word and with no prop besides a cup of water.

It was 11:15 by the time the sound came back (a blown amplifier was later blamed) and Carter went back to his answer:

> There has been too much government secrecy and not enough respect for the personal privacy of American citizens.

It would be the last question of the debate.

Mime Beating on South Street

1988

For a few days in 1988, outside of the International House on the University of Pennsylvania campus, there was a chalk outline of Leo Bassi's body. Next to it, an empty pedestal stood as a monument to a fallen clown.

Bassi, a household name in his native Italy, specialized in outrageous public performance. On one occasion, with the permission of the local police and mayor of an Italian town, Bassi staged a bank robbery complete with car chases and shoot outs. In other cases, he used bulldozers, airplanes, and fire departments for his curious brand of street theater.

Upon arriving in Philadelphia as part of the Movement Theatre International Festival, Bassi asked where in town he was most likely to find creative energy. He was pointed in the direction of South Street.

So on June 4, in the midst of packed Saturday night

Personal interview with participants.

220

gawkers, Bassi and his assistants picked a spot between Fifth and Sixth streets, one of the city's busiest blocks. They set up a five-foot pedestal and Bassi climbed aboard, yuppified in a suit and overcoat and carrying a briefcase. He tilted a light from a nearby building so that he was in the spotlight and then proceeded to strike poses. Occasionally he would break out of this statue character to razz his audience by making faces and squirting a watergun. Curious crowds gathered. Cars driving by slowed down. "Who is that crazy man?" someone asked.

Things got more confusing when, while Bassi was posing declaratively with a finger pointed skyward, a stranger tried to grab the briefcase. Bassi reacted quickly and grabbed the case. The stranger then grabbed Bassi's coattails and pulled the stout performer off his pedestal and down to the ground, where he landed on his shoulder.

Robert Shields, of the well-known Shields and Yarnell mime team, along with other pamphleteers from the Movement Theater Festival, rushed to the fallen man as the stranger rushed into the crowd. The audience pushed closer, trying to figure out if this was part of Bassi's act. While the police converged, Shields climbed onto the pedestal to announce that this was not part of the show and that Bassi was actually hurt pretty badly.

While Bassi waited to be taken to the hospital, some civic minding onlookers told him not to judge Philly by this. Others said it served him right. A pair of guys wearing gold chains said they would "kick the attacker's ass." Not having access to the attacker, they instead took a pile of brochures and said they would tell all their friends to go to Bassi's show.

The bewildered Bassi was taken in a police car to Einstein Hospital, where he was treated for a dislocated shoulder. The injury forced him to rethink the program for his show, The New Neuronian, which was scheduled to open that evening. Having use of only one arm left only about twenty minutes of the show—including juggling a couch with his feet.

Bassi was still in pain when he spoke to his performance class two days later. He stressed to his students that, far from making a mistake in taking on South Street, he had in fact found the right place to perform. He said:

> Performance and theater and culture is dead. In order to make it come alive maybe we need to be thrown around a bit. ❧

The Color of Money
1989

Douglas Miller and Mike Ryan were in the process of printing half a million dollars worth of $10,000 bills when word came that the Feds were on their way. Soon, a knock came to the door of their North Delaware Avenue office. It was Secret Service Agent Jack Rodeschin. He wasn't smiling.

Miller and Ryan never saw themselves as forgers. Their ten-year-old business, Holographic Design, had become one of the largest manufacturers of holograms in the country. It was Ryan's idea to capture the holographic image of a $10,000 bill, frame it, and sell it as a gag gift item. They borrowed the rare bill from a Louisiana collector and, through the magic of laser photography, captured the three-dimensional image on glass. Ryan had already consulted with an assistant DA he knew in Salt Lake City who assured him there would be no problem with the government as long as no one tried to cash the bill (which would have been difficult since it would disappear if the glass were cracked). Gift retailer The Sharper Image showed an interest in the product, ordered sixteen hundred of the holograms, and featured it in its catalog. Response was outstanding. A week after the catalog was distributed, The Sharper Image called and ordered twenty thousand more, the largest order Ryan and Miller ever had.

But then the Feds heard about it. An 1895 federal statute states that it is illegal to create an exact reproduction or facsimile of u.s. currency. According to the law, any reproduction has to be 75 percent smaller or 150 percent larger than the original and in black and white. The $10,000 bill hologram did not meet those criteria (a hologram can only be created in color and on a one-to-one scale).

The Feds admitted after seeing the operation that Miller and Ryan were not deliberately breaking the law. No charges were filed, and even Agent Rodeschin agreed that it would be impossible to cash or spend the hologram. But the law was clear. The agent asked if there was a place nearby where they could dispose of the remaining pieces. They were destroyed and the holographers decided not to fight the case. ✄